Owning

Model S

The Definitive Guide to Buying and Owning the Tesla Model S

2nd Edition

Nick J Howe

Copyright and Notices

In memory of Joan Howe

Table Of Contents

Foreword

The Tesla Model S is a very special car. Special—because it represents a discontinuity in the history of modern automobiles. Special—because it proves that premium electric vehicles can compete and win in looks, performance, and safety against the best car brands in the world. Special—because, well, because I own one.

I'm a very early adopter of the Model S (VIN #184) and met Nick Howe before either of us owned the car. Both of us studied every early report on the Model S, commented in the forums about everything from the car's elegant design to the first guesstimates of delivery dates and pricing.

During the wait, and after his car was delivered, Nick took the broad view, delving into all things Model S and becoming expert in many of them. He became recognized and respected on the forums as a guy who knew the car, its features, its functions, and its idiosyncrasies.

My journey was a bit different. I became interested in the interior of the car, designing and building what I viewed as a necessary accessory for the interior. Our company, which you can check out at evannex.com, grew out of that early work. We're proud to publish the second edition of Nick's book, **Owning Model S.**

All Model S owners "discover" the car, both before they take delivery and after it sits in their driveway. Model S owners try to understand what for many is their first electric vehicle. They want to be sure this 21st century automobile is right for them. Those who decide to pull the trigger want to pick the right options before they take delivery. They want to appreciate what to expect during their first week of ownership. They want to learn the tricks that will make them become Model S experts as quickly as possible.

With this book, Nick Howe has satisfied all of those "wants." He'll help you to better understand the technology, better decide whether the car is right for you, better choose the right options, better appreciate the car's many features and functions, and drive the car during your first few weeks as if you've owned it for a year. Applying his voluminous knowledge of the Model S, Nick has expanded and updated his very popular first edition, and provides up-to-date information on the world's best car. In so doing, he has done a wonderful service for the Tesla community.

Owning Model S is a must-have for every person who is considering the Model S and every driver who currently owns one.

Roger Pressman

Preface

Imagine a five-seat luxury sedan. Leather and veneer interior. Smooth. Quiet. Refined. Now imagine that it can do zero-to-sixty in less than three seconds yet is the safest car in America. Sounds like a car that many drivers would aspire to own.

Now imagine that it has the fuel economy of a small motorcycle. And that it gets free upgrades every month, without visiting the dealer. And can travel long distances for free, forever, on sunlight.

Not science fiction. Not something from the future. This is Tesla Motors' *Model S*, available today.

It was never my intention to write this book. I have a full-time job. I have a family. I have more than enough to keep me busy. But I also have a Tesla Model S—Pearl White, Grey wheels, Performance 85. We call her "Sparky."

I took delivery in January 2013—two years, one month and twelve days after placing my order. Back in 2010 when I placed my order, Model S was a distant dream—the "alpha" prototype existed, but we didn't know if it would ever enter production.

In October 2011, I was at the factory when Elon Musk drove the first beta car onto the stage and announced to the world that this thing was *real*. And boy, is it real! Model S is in many ways like every car you've ever owned, but in many other ways it's like nothing you've ever owned.

In the four years since I placed the order, and in the two years since I took delivery, I've learned much about Model S, been asked and have answered many questions and seen many statements made (quite a few of them incorrect) about the car, the battery, charging, range...the list goes on.

That's why I wrote this book—to share my experiences and to help you make the most of something that is so familiar, yet so different.

This book sets out to dispel the myths that surround this engineering marvel, and to help you through the journey of evaluating, configuring, and ultimately owning Model S.

I learn something new every day, and am constantly updating **OwningModelS.com**, the website that accompanies this book. If you have any feedback please contact me there, or via the Tesla Motors forum, or via email at **info@OwningModelS.com**.

Welcome to the future of motoring.

Conventions used in this book

Throughout this book I'll use the term **ICE** (short for internal combustion engine) to describe fossil fuel (gas, petrol, diesel, natural gas) cars, **Hybrid** for both plug-in and extended-range electric-ICE cars, and **BEV** (Battery Electric Vehicle) to describe cars such as Model S.

If you see the word **battery** on its own I'm referring to the main drive battery (also known as the *battery pack*. I'll always say **12V battery** if I'm referring specifically to that.

Second Edition

This is the second edition of *Owning Model S*, fully updated through August 2015 to reflect the dual-motor variants, the addition of autopilot capability, and the other myriad changes introduced to Model S during its first three years.

Acknowledgements

I'd like to thank the many hundreds of members of the Tesla Motors and Tesla Motors Club forums without whose questions, answers, and support this book would never have been possible, especially @Musterion, @shop, @jat@jaet.org, @DouglasR, Bill Hart (@Lolachampcar), Jay Todtman (@jtodtman), Craig Froehle (@cfOH) and Michael Greco. Names of other owners who helped with this book are included in the Index.

Tommy Bombon is a fantastic photographer and long time friend. His portfolio is at https://www.facebook.com/atomicBeeProductions. Quite a number of the photos in this book are his.

Scott Lefler is a budding graphic designer who helped design or redesign a number of the figures in this book. He's also happens to be my step-son.

I'd especially like to thank Roger Pressman (@soflauthor) for creating the original "delivery checklist" that started the whole thing, for his suggestion that I take my accumulated wisdom and put pen to paper (or rather finger to MacBook), and for his assistance in bringing this book to market.

Finally I'd like to thank my wife, Linda, who agreed to let me spend six figures on a car she'd never seen, let alone ridden in. I love her dearly.

Nick Howe
Boca Raton, FL

1 In the Beginning

The Visionary

In 2004, Elon Musk invested $6.3 million in a startup called "Tesla Motors" and set out to change the future of the global automotive industry. Tesla Motors was, and is, the embodiment of his vision to accelerate the mainstream adoption of sustainable transport, and Model S is the platform on which that vision will be realized.

©TommyBombon /atomicBee

Much has been written about Elon Musk, and I don't intend to repeat it all here. As CEO, Chief Product Architect and force behind Tesla Motors, Elon has been compared to Apple's Steve Jobs—a driven entrepreneur, a creative genius, and a technological visionary. Calling someone a *visionary* is often viewed as hype; in the case of Elon Musk, it's a statement of fact.

At college he determined to focus on the three things that would, in his opinion, most affect the future of humanity. These were the Internet, sustainable energy, and humanity becoming a multi-planet species. These thoughts led to his key roles in X.com (which became PayPal), SolarCity and Tesla Motors (sustainable energy production and consumption, respectively), and SpaceX.

Tesla Motors _____

Elon often captures the headlines, but considerably less has been written about how *Model S* came to be. Many people believe that Elon started Tesla Motors and he is acknowledged as a co-founder of the company. But in reality he didn't join until 2004. Martin Eberhard and Marc Tarpenning started the original company in 2003 in San Carlos, California to mass-produce AC Propulsion's *tzero* concept car, powered by Lithium-ion batteries.

Upon joining Tesla Motors, Elon set out to transform the company into something much greater. In 2006 Elon wrote:

> "...the overarching purpose of Tesla Motors (and the reason I am funding the company) is to help expedite the move from a mine-and-burn hydrocarbon economy towards a solar electric economy..." [1]

He quickly established a three-step business plan:

Step 1: Build a low volume, high cost electric car as a development platform. Code named *DarkStar*, the result was *Roadster*, launched in 2008.

Step 2: Take the lessons learned from Step 1 and build a mid-volume, premium car. Code named *WhiteStar*, the result was the *Model S*, launched in 2012 (and the *Model X* SUV, launched in 2015.)

Step 3: Take the lessons from Step 2, incorporate advances in battery technology, and build a high volume, low-cost car. Code-named *BlueStar*, it is targeted to be launched in late 2017 and planned to be called *Model 3*.

The goal (at least for Elon) was not to build a successful car company *per se*, but to prove to the large auto markers that it was possible to create a successful, sustainable, electric car company, thereby spurring them to enter the market more aggressively than they would otherwise do.

_____

[1] http://www.teslamotors.com/blog/secret-tesla-motors-master-plan-just-between-you-and-me

The Early Years

During Step 1, Tesla designed and built its own power electronics, motor and other drivetrain components after initially licensing them from AC Propulsion. Entering into an agreement with Lotus Cars in 2005 to purchase Lotus' rolling chassis, Tesla produced several prototypes of Roadster before it finally entered production in March 2008.

Roadster is an amazing two-seater, all-electric sports car, loosely based on the Lotus Elise. The Roadster program enabled Tesla to perfect the basic energy storage and control systems that would be crucial for later steps in Elon's strategy. The car was very high performance, belying the notion that battery electric vehicles were stodgy.

With a target production run of 1,700 cars over three years (subsequently raised to 2,400),[2] Roadster was deliberately aimed at a very limited audience. Despite this, it created a lot of buzz and put Tesla Motors on the map.

The Inside Story of Model S

Step 2 spanned a period of almost five years and drove Tesla Motors close to bankruptcy. Model S is Tesla's first car designed from the ground up and developed for large-scale production for the general automotive marketplace. In common with the approach taken by many other auto manufacturers, Model S is not just a car, but also a *platform* on which other cars—such as the Model X[3]—will be based.

As Model S progressed from a rough idea to a production vehicle, it was not without its detractors. In fact, executives in the old-school auto industry and the "experts" who populated the automotive and financial media thought Tesla Motors was a bad joke and Model S was "vaporware."

Bob Lutz, ex-Vice-Chairman of General Motors, speaking in 2012: "Bottom line: Tesla produces a nice car for a social elite that can afford $80–110K transportation. That's a thin market, where innovation is rewarded, but prone to being discarded with equal speed when the next must-have "gold Rolex" comes along. Don't confuse it with what Detroit does for a living."[4]

---

[2] The original plan was to produce 1,700 Roadsters from the total of 1,700 Elise "gliders" (cars with no powertrain) that Lotus had available. Tesla subsequently purchased the final 700 gliders that Lotus built before they ended their production run due to factory retooling.
[3] The Model X is a premium SUV that is the next ground-up offering from Tesla Motors.
[4] http://www.forbes.com/sites/boblutz/2012/07/13/tesla-beating-detroit-thats-just-nonsense/

Mitt Romney, during the 2012 presidential debate, called Tesla a "loser."[5]

Eric Jackson, founder and president of Ironfire Capital: "I'm short Tesla and [...] think it could be the next Webvan."[6,7]

Anyone taking a cursory look at the Tesla financial picture in the middle of 2012 might have jumped to similar conclusions:

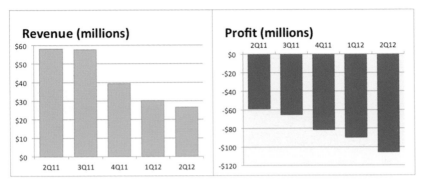

Figure 1 Tesla Motors 2nd Quarter 2012 GAAP Revenue and Profit

Revenues were falling, and losses were mounting. This wasn't the first time Tesla's financials had been in a dire position. Towards the end of 2008 the company was, to quote Elon, "an hour away from bankruptcy". At 6:00pm on Christmas Eve in 2008 Elon sunk everything he had into Tesla Motors and convinced his key partners to match his investment. Had he not done this, the company would have "gone bankrupt a few days after Christmas." Five months later Daimler AG bought a 10% stake in Tesla and enabled Tesla to move forward with the Roadster program.[8]

What isn't obvious from Figure 1 is that Roadster production had just ended, and Model S production was just starting. The turn around in financial fortunes was beginning:

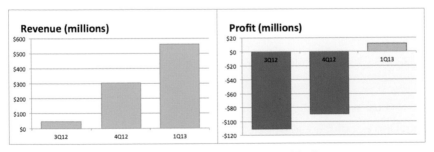

Figure 2 Tesla Motors 1st Quarter 2013 GAAP Revenue and Profit

[5] http://www.huffingtonpost.com/2012/10/04/mitt-romney-tesla_n_1939531.html
[6] Webvan was a dot-com failure, losing hundreds of millions of dollars of venture capital and IPO funding.
[7] http://www.thestreet.com/story/10838464/2/why-tesla-is-the-next-webvan.html
[8] http://www.teslamotors.com/about/press/releases/strategic-partnership-daimler-acquires-stake-tesla

Six months after the announcement of the Model S concept, Tesla Motors nearly went bankrupt, yet only three and a half years later the first Model S rolled off the production line in a new state-of-the-art factory.

Model S Prototype. Alpha and Beta vehicles at the Tesla Factory (with the Motor Trend 2013 Car of the Year award)

SUMMARY TIMELINE:

- **June 30, 2008**: Model S is announced via a press release
- **March 26, 2009**: the prototype Model S is displayed at a press conference
- **May 2010**: Tesla announces Model S will be built at the former NUMMI plant in Fremont, California
- **June 2010**: Tesla floats on the NASDAQ, raising $226 million
- **October 2011**: Elon drives the Model S beta onto the stage at the factory, to cheers from hundreds of reservation holders and employees
- **June 22, 2012**: the first ten "Founders" cars roll off the production line
- **August 11, 2012**: Signature #1 (of 1000) is delivered to Jason Calacanis
- **August 7, 2013**: first Model S deliveries outside North America start (Norway)
- **January 2014**: Nearly 22,500 Model S were delivered in 2013
- **February 2015**: Over 31,600 Model S were delivered in 2014[9]

In three years since its launch, Model S has racked up over one billion miles[9] and won *hundreds* of awards[10] including:

- **2013 *Motor Trend* Car of the Year**
- ***Automobile Magazine's* 2013 Car of the Year**
- ***Consumer Reports'* top-scoring car ever, Most Loved Car, and #1 for service and repairs**
- ***National Highway Traffic Safety Administration (NHTSA)* top ranked five star safety rating**

[9] 1Q 2015 Shareholder letter
[10] http://my.teslamotors.com/forum/forums/tesla-timeline-0

2 The Car and Its Revolutionary Tech

The World's Best Car

Elon Musk firmly believed that the lack of mainstream adoption of battery electric cars was because car companies had framed the problem incorrectly. With Model S, Tesla set out not to build the world's best *electric* car, but the world's best car.

My Pearl White P85, "Sparky'

To be the best car in the world, Model S needed to:

*   have a driving range comparable to internal combustion engine cars

*   seat five adults comfortably

*   have performance comparable to the best German sedans

*   have industry-leading safety

*   have class-leading luggage capacity

*   have aesthetic appeal across a broad spectrum of buyers

Model S is a classic example of the principle "form follows function." The overall design and packaging of the car meet critical engineering goals (e.g., luggage capacity, range, performance) and at the same time achieve an overall aesthetic that is stunning. For example, the engineering design choices for battery placement and the need for a low drag coefficient (see discussion of drag later in this chapter) led to excellent handling and flowing lines.

This mixture of beautiful design *and* state-of-the-art engineering was at least in part accomplished by co-locating the design and engineering teams in a corner of the SpaceX facility in Southern California.[11] The interplay of the two groups and constant iteration meant that form and function evolved together.

Plug and Go

Arguably, the relatively poor market penetration of battery electric cars is directly related to the public's concern about where to charge—specifically a *lack* of places to charge. This generates what is known as "range anxiety."

> The first question about electric cars is usually, "what happens if I run out of charge?" The term "range anxiety" is often used to describe this concern.

To alleviate range anxiety, driving and refuelling Model S would have to be at least comparable to a gasoline car. 300 miles of range from a single charge was chosen as a design goal, and to achieve that goal, two key design elements had to be addressed: *vehicle drag* and *vehicle weight.*

DRAG AND MODEL S

Image © Tesla Motors, used with permission.

Above about 45 mph the biggest single factor that affects fuel consumption in any car—regardless of what form of energy it uses—is the "wind

---

[11] http://gigaom.com/2013/11/06/how-tesla-overcame-the-challenges-of-electric-car-design-from-the-ground-up/

resistance", known technically as "aerodynamic drag." A primary engineering and design challenge for any car is therefore to make it "slippery." That is, to minimize aerodynamic drag, thereby improving range. This is as true for Model S as it is for any internal combustion engine (ICE) car.

But what does "reducing aerodynamic drag" mean, really? And why is it important?

The air that we breathe is invisible and insubstantial. As we walk down the street we hardly notice that our bodies push the air out of the way, but as objects travel faster the effort needed to keep pushing the air away grows dramatically. A tractor-trailer moving down the freeway at 60 mph is moving one ton of air out of the way every 6 seconds! Moving that air requires effort, and effort requires energy and reduces range. Further, the effort goes up with the speed squared—so if the speed is doubled, you'll need four times the effort to move the air out of the way. To maximize range (at any given speed) you need to minimize the effort needed to move the air out of the way. That is what the phrase "minimizing drag" really means.

Air flows around some shapes better than others and hence different shapes have different drag. Drag is measured by a "drag coefficient", shown by the symbol "c_d."

> Simply put, c_d is a measure of how easily air (or any fluid) flows around an object. If the air flows twice as easily, we have half the drag and hence half the effort is needed to maintain a given speed. The lower the c_d the better.

Here are the c_d values for a range of objects:

• Truck	0.6-1.0
• Dodge Viper RT/10	0.45
• Cadillac Escalade Hybrid	0.36
• Ford Taurus	0.30
• Toyota Prius (2001)	0.29
• Lexus LS460	0.26
• Toyota Prius (2014)	0.25
• Tesla Model S	0.24
• General Motors EV1 (1996)	0.195

Low drag is crucial to fuel efficiency. When Model S was released it had the lowest drag coefficient (c_d of 0.24) of any production car.

Even after more than 10 years of development, the Toyota Prius continues to have a higher c_d than the first generation Model S.

To achieve its incredibly low c_d, you'll notice that Model S has a number of important design features:

- A "Fastback" shape (vs a traditional "three-box" shape). Low drag requires smooth air flow. Anything that increases turbulence (represented as spirals in the figure) increases drag.

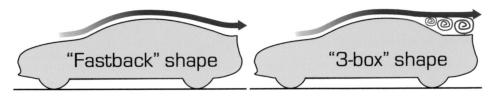

- A flat underside—typically seen in race cars—again to reduce turbulence. The Model S with air suspension dynamically lowers itself at speed to further reduce turbulence.
- Retractable door handles. (In reality this is more cosmetic than aerodynamic, but it does help slightly.)

Wing mirrors increase drag by approximately 3%. The prototype Tesla Model X did away with external mirrors in favor of small high definition cameras. Current US regulations prohibit this approach, but Tesla is lobbying to change this.

- A rounded nose cone. The ideal low drag shape is a teardrop, with a cd of 0.05. The rounded nose and the overall rounded profile of the front of the car helps Model S get closer to the teardrop shape.
- A rear diffuser. You may have noticed the chrome-edged "tunnel" at the rear of the car. This "diffuser" funnels the air from the underside and lowers its pressure, thereby reducing turbulence at the rear of the car. It also has the beneficial effect of creating "downforce", making the car more stable at high speeds.

Model S Rear Diffuser and Flat Underside

As a consequence of these features, Model S is a "slippery" car, and that's part of the reason that it achieves such excellent range.

WEIGHT AND MODEL S

Below 45 mph, the majority of drag comes from the "rolling resistance" of the tires, and is directly proportional to the weight of the car. A 10% reduction in weight equals a 10% improvement in range. Given its relatively heavy batteries, it was imperative to reduce the weight of the rest of the car. Most of that weight is in the chassis and body, so Tesla looked to replace the heavy steel typically used in production cars with a lighter weight material. Tesla had to accomplish this without compromising the rigidity and crash protection of the car, so it chose aluminum instead of steel for the main structure, with steel inserts where necessary for enhanced crash protection.

Model S aluminum structure.
Image © Tesla Motors. Used with permission.

"For limited or low-volume production cars like the Roadster, carbon fiber is a great material to reduce weight. It's not a solution for higher-volume production due to cost and manufacturing time. For Model S, we are using aluminum for the body panels and chassis. Aluminum is as strong as steel but lighter in weight, and has similar manufacturing capabilities. Lighter weight translates directly to efficiency." Tesla Chief Designer Franz von Holzhausen[12]

Aluminum's major benefit is that it is only one third the weight of steel, but it introduces a number of challenges to the manufacturing process. Aluminum is much more difficult to weld than steel, requiring the use of robotic precision welding equipment. In addition, aluminum is not magnetic. Rolls of aluminum sheet enter the factory, and are then cut and stamped prior to

Aluminum roll at the Tesla factory

welding. The robots that had moved the sheet metal around in the NUMMI factory that Tesla Motors took over to produce Model S used powerful electromagnets to lift the steel; these robots had to be retrofitted with vacuum suction units to perform the same actions on aluminum.[13]

For owners, the most noticable impact of aluminum when operating Model S is the relative lack of stiffness of the hood, requiring the "two-handed-push" approach to latching it (to avoid denting it).

[12] http://www.teslamotors.com/blog/model-s-designing-perfect-endurance-athlete
[13] More information on the Tesla Factory and Model S production process is presented in the next chapter.

The Electric Powertrain

Model S is a *battery electric vehicle* (BEV). Unlike hybrids or plug-in hybrids, there is no internal combustion engine and no gasoline tank or fuel cell.

> The biggest and by far the most fundamental difference between Model S and every other car in its class is the electric powertrain. The powertrain includes the battery, the inverter and the motor.

The components of the Model S battery system and powertrain are:

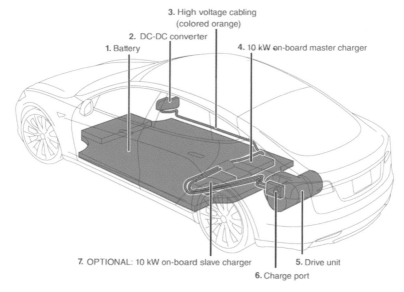

3. High voltage cabling (colored orange)
2. DC-DC converter
1. Battery
4. 10 kW on-board master charger
7. OPTIONAL: 10 kW on-board slave charger
5. Drive unit
6. Charge port

Figure 3 Model S charging and powertrain subsystems. Image © Tesla Motors. Used with permission.

To understand how these components work together I'll take a short and (I promise) not-too-technical detour into some basic electrical concepts.

First of all, it's important to understand that there are two different ways in which electricity can flow—Direct Current (DC) and Alternating Current (AC)—and that DC can be converted to AC, and vice versa. For the purposes of this discussion it is sufficient to know that they *are* different, without going into the differences. It is also important to note that they each have their pros and cons, and that Model S uses both AC and DC.

Here are a few examples of components that use AC and some that use DC:

Alternating Current (AC)	Direct Current (DC)
110-400 V household supply	12V battery
J1772 chargers	Main (traction) battery
High Power Wall Connector	Car instruments and lights
Main Drive Motor(s)[14]	Tesla Superchargers
	CHAdeMO chargers

Referring to Figure 3 above, the *charger* (4) converts AC to DC. The *inverter* (contained within the drive unit, 5) converts DC to AC. The **DC–DC converter** (2) connects the 366V battery to the 12V battery.

The Traction Battery and The "Skateboard"

At the heart of Model S is the main battery pack, known as the "traction battery". Sitting between the two axles it is part of the structure of the car, but can be removed and replaced in less than two minutes.

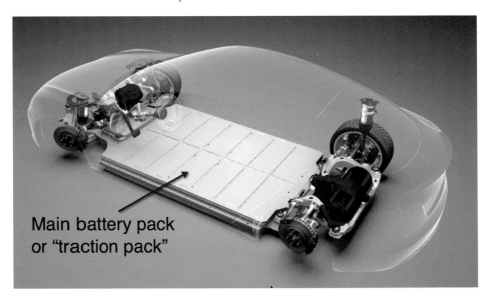

Main battery pack or "traction pack"

It contains over 7000 individual "lithium-ion" battery cells wired together, and weighs roughly 1000 lbs.

Placing the battery pack as a structual member in the floor pan of the car lowered the center of gravity—dramatically reducing body roll compared to

[14] It should be noted that the first patent for an AC induction motor was granted in 1888 to Nikola Tesla, after whom Tesla Motors is named. Throughout this book I use "Tesla" to refer to Tesla Motors.

ICE cars. It also created a "skateboard" design that would allow other body styles to be developed with relatively little work.

Model S Skateboard

> The skateboard design, combined with the lack of an engine in the front of the car and the small motor and inverter mounted between the rear wheels, means no center tunnel running through the passenger compartment and huge amounts of cargo space. Consequently Model S has the more cargo space than just about any car and many SUVs.

An aside: The Gigafactory

In the next chapter we'll discuss Tesla's state-of-the-art factory in which Model S is built, but since we were just talking about batteries it is worth taking a short detour to discuss the "Gigafactory".

Each Model S uses approximately 7000 individual battery cells. Model 3 (Tesla's mid-market car) launches in 2017, and by 2020 Tesla's goal is to produce roughly half a million cars per year. Although there may be fewer cells in each Model 3, Tesla will still need something like 2.5 *billion* cells per year. This is roughly the *entire world's production* of lithium-ion cells in 2013.

How does Tesla double global cell production in only five years? Tesla is very keen on "vertical integration"—meaning it owns many of the processes in the entire manufacturing supply chain for Model S—and so took the massive step of bringing battery production in-house. It decided to build its own battery factory, partnering with its current battery cell supplier Panasonic. After reviewing sites in several states, Tesla settled on a location outside Reno, Nevada and started construction on one of the largest buildings in the world.

Gigafactory construction site. Image © Bob Tregilus. Used with permission. CC BY-NC-SAR 4.0

The factory is truly huge. 24 million square feet, equivalent to 500 football pitches. It is due to come online in March 2016 and at full capacity will produce nearly 3 billion cells per year.

Rendering of the completed factory. Image © Tesla Motors. Used with permission.

It will include a battery recycling plant and massive solar energy farm. Completed traction packs will be transported by rail to the Fremont car factory. And now back to Model S.

Regenerative Braking

Instead of using its brakes Model S can use the motor to slow the car down, and in doing so puts energy back into the battery. This simple statement highlights one of the biggest differences of Model S from an ICE car.

From your school science class you might remember that, "energy can be transformed from one form to another, but cannot be created or destroyed." When a car accelerates, the powertrain converts the chemical energy in the fuel to what physicists call "kinetic energy"—the energy that a body possesses as a result of its motion. When you slow down, that kinetic energy has to go somewhere. In an old-technology ICE car, friction in the brakes converts kinetic energy to heat energy—which is why brakes become very hot after braking—you may have seen the glowing brakes on racecars. All of this kinetic energy is therefore lost to the environment—it is wasted. In Model S, the energy is harvested and returned to the battery.

When an electrical current is applied to the Model S motor it creates a magnetic field that causes the motor to spin, moving the car. When Model S is moving *without* a current being applied (slowing down or going downhill), the motor *generates* a current, which in turn generates a magnetic field. The magnetic field slows the motor (and the car) down, and the induced current charges the battery. The kinetic energy (speed) is converted to magnetic, then electrical, then chemical energy in the battery. This process *regenerates* electricity.

> Regen (electricity regeneration) is the recovery of energy (and hence range) by converting the car's speed (kinetic energy) to electrical current and ultimately chemical energy in the battery. All of this occurs when the car decelerates.

In Model S this happens automatically when you lift off of the accelerator pedal, whereas in some hybrids and BEVs pressing the brake pedal activates regen. The Model S system is much more elegant and gives a much smoother ride. In contrast, the typical hybrid car approach of trying to balance physical braking and regen to slow the car down smoothly is difficult to get right.

Q. How much kinetic energy does it recapture?

The conversion of kinetic energy to chemical (battery) energy during deceleration can be as high as 80% efficient. In other words if you used 1 kilowatt-hour (kWh) of battery energy accelerating to 100 mph, and you were to immediately slow down to zero using only regen you would find that by the time you came to rest your total energy use could be as little as 0.2 kWh.

Q. Can you really use regen instead of the brakes?

Most owners find that with the regen set to "standard" (rather than "low") it is sufficiently powerful that using the brake pedal is not necessary during normal driving. You'll only need the brakes for  the last few feet when bringing the car to a complete stop, or to hold the car at rest on an incline.

Q. Regen felt strange during my test drive. Will I get used to it?

Most definitely! Most drivers adjust within a few minutes of driving the car. In fact after adjusting to "one-foot driving" (press to accelerate, lift to decelerate), most drivers find the need to use brakes in regular cars quite frustrating and antiquated.

The Frunk

One of the small delights of Model S is the front trunk or "frunk". With the motor roughly the size of a watermelon and mounted between the wheels there's no need for an large engine up front. A fun pastime is to show people the trunk, then to open the hood and wait for the obvious question, "Where's the engine?"

A Software Defined Experience_____

In 1986 Buick introduced the computer first touch screen into its Riviera model, and since then many manufacturers have incorporated the technology, but no one has done it like Tesla.

THE 17-INCH TOUCHSCREEN

In a radical move, Tesla did away with the dozens of buttons that typically litter a car dashboard. Instead, they used an industry-first 17-inch touch sensitive display mounted on the dashboard between the driver and passenger, plus a smaller screen for the instrument cluster. The speedometer and other displays are implemented in software, along with the user interface for many of the car's controls.

Image © Tesla Motors. Used with permission.

The screen is remarkably easy to use and, surprising to many people when first seeing it, is not a distraction when driving. The only physical controls are the turn signals, wiper controls, cruise control, hazard warning lights, and the glove compartment. Everything else is initiated via the touchscreen. Seeing satellite-based maps on the 17" display is quite amazing.

This software-based approach was further enhanced by the introduction of "over-the-air software downloads" that periodically provide enhancements to both the user interface and to the features of the car.

THE TESLA SMARTPHONE APP

A discussion of Model S software wouldn't be complete without mentioning the Tesla Model S app available on iPhone and Android.

The app enables you to control charging, control heating and cooling, lock and unlock, flash the lights, honk the horn, and track the location and (should the car be moving) its speed, from anywhere in the world. It is great for turning on the heater or A/C to get the car ready before you drive, or to check whether the charging is complete.

A Car That Improves With Age

One of the benefits of having most functionality implemented in software rather than via physical buttons is that the layout can be tweaked and improved over time, and functions can be improved *or even added*.

Here are some of the new or improved features introduced over several software versions:

- Version 1.17 (a.k.a. V4, Nov 2012)—Sleep mode. Voice commands. Auto-presenting door handles. Alarm. Range driving mode. USB Media browsing. Sunroof control via steering wheel. Location-aware Homelink. Energy app. Throttle response.

- Version 5.0 (Aug 2013)—Wi-Fi support and cell phone tethering. Audio controls improvements. Maps oriented to direction of travel. Sleep mode improvements. Smoother low speed creep. Support for the new cold weather package.

- Version 5.6 (Oct 2013)—Audio controls improvements. New voice-over languages. Maps improvements. Improvements to range calculations.
- Version 6.0 (Sep 2014) —Traffic-based navigation. On-screen calendar. New power management options. Location-based smart air suspension

Note the first item—throttle response. Model S P85 was originally quoted as having a 4.4 second 0 to 60 time. With version 1.17 software Tesla tweaked the throttle response mapping for the inverter/motor and *reduced the 0 to 60 time to 4.2 seconds!*

Do you know any other cars that give you free, over-the-air performance improvements?

Remember that every Model S produced has been able to take advantage of these improvements. No need to wait for the next model year!

Although Tesla is generally tight-lipped about future software updates, various features have been hinted at or promised:

- Version 7.0, due in late summer 2015, is expected to enable the "highway autosteer" functionality (see the section below on autopilot).
- We expect to see web browser performance improvements when Tesla switches from a proprietary web browser to Chrome.
- Various hints have been dropped about allowing owners to personalize the look and feel of the screen controls, and about support for third party applications.

Autopilot

When Model S was first introduced, the biggest criticism was the lack of driver aids. Compared with similarly priced Mercedes, BMWs, Porsches, or even Hyundais at a fraction of the Model S price, Model S was seriously disadvantaged. No adaptive cruise control, no heads-up display, no lane departure warning—in fact no driver aids whatsoever—not even parking sensors.

This all changed when a suite of sensor hardware was added to Model S. Starting in late September 2014, all new cars were equipped with a forward-looking camera, radar, and 360-degree ultrasonic sensors.

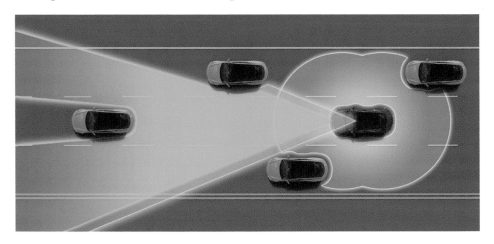

Image © Tesla Motors. Used with permission.

Starting with software version 6.1, features were added to take advantage of these sensors. At the time of writing, traffic-aware cruise control, forward collision warning, and auto high beam had been enabled, but in October 2014 at the launch of the dual motor P85D variant of Model S, Tesla demonstrated true hands-free driving including automatic lane changing, with it scheduled to appear in software version 7.0 in late summer of 2015. Along with "highway autosteer", Elon has said the software will include a driverless 'self-parking' feature where the car will park itself *after the driver has exited the car*.

Dual Motor All-Wheel Drive

The Model S was released initially as a rear-wheel drive car, but in October 2014 Tesla introduced the S60D[15], S85D, and P85D variants. These cars incorporated a second electric motor driving the front wheels.

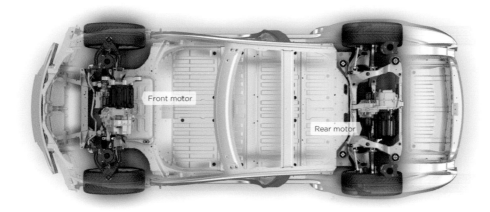

The massive torque of the electric motors, combined with the near instantaneous fine control of the drive-by-wire power train gives unparalleled acceleration, and exceptional road holding in slippery driving conditions.

In the most extreme case, the P85D develops a combined 691 hp and is capable of zero to sixty miles per hour in 2.8[16] seconds, beating Elon's design goal of matching the time of the famed $1 million McLaren F1 that he bought after selling his startup company Zip2.

The Final Result

Every aspect of Model S came under intense scutiny by the automotive community and media. As I noted earlier, many said the entire design was a pipe dream, others said the idea was a good one, but the implementation would be a disaster. Still others argued that the design was solid but the car couldn't be built at any reasonable price point. They were all wrong.

Tesla demolished each of these concerns one-by-one, and Model S has become an automotive phenomenon.

---

[15] The S60D was removed from sale almost immediately when Tesla simplified the range line up. It was later replaced by the S70D. See Chapter 5, Configuring and Ordering for more details about the different models.
[16] P85D with Ludicrous Mode

OWNING MODEL S

3 The Factory and Charging Infrastructure

Producing Model S

The original intention was to build Model S in New Mexico, but a meeting between Akio Toyoda, President of Toyota, and Elon Musk led to a remarkable outcome: Toyota would sell the 380-acre GM/Toyota New United Motor Manufacturing, Inc. (NUMMI) plant in Fremont, California to Tesla for $42 million[17], and simultaneously invest $50 million in Tesla. This essentially provided Tesla a ready-made 5.4 million sq. ft. factory capable of producing 400,000 cars-per-year, for free.

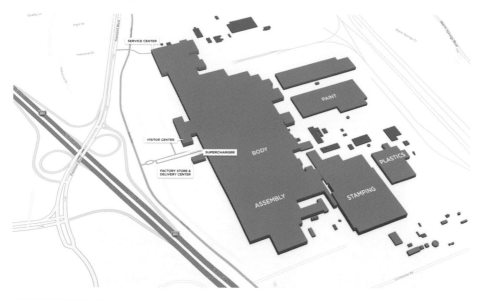

[17] http://venturebeat.com/2010/05/27/tesla-paid-42m-for-nummi-but-doesnt-have-deal-to-build-cars-with-toyota/

Or rather the factory was *almost capable*. Significant retooling was required, along with a brand new robotic assemby line including:

The largest hydraulic presses in North America (7 stories tall)...

A state of the art robotic paint shop and drying station...

(which is being replaced by an even *more* state-of-the art paint shop costing $650 million)

A state of the art robotic assembly line using robots from manufacturer KUKA...

Even an injection molding facility for body panels...

In August of 2014, Tesla shut down production for two weeks to install a brand new production line capable of over 2,000 cars per week for Model S and Model X. If you have further interest, details of the factory and Model S production process can be seen in the National Geographic documentary *Mega Factories*, available on YouTube.

Building a Charging Infrastructure for Electric Cars _____

When I tell someone I drive an electric car, I can pretty much guarantee that the first thing out of their mouth will be, "What happens if it runs out of charge?"

This is a natural question. Whether in Chicago or Istanbul, drivers are used to seeing a gas station on almost every corner. Electric charging stations? Not so much.

This "filling the tank" element of the automotive infrastucture is being re-created for BEVs like Model S. But Tesla did not start from scratch. There are already many more charging locations than most people realize. In fact the website PlugShare.com shows over 20,000 charging locations in North America:

From PlugShare www.plugshare.com © 2014 Recargo, Inc.

Roadster owners and the "early adopters" among us—those that put a deposit down on a car that only existed in prototype form and on the drawing board—carefully considered and understood what would be required to live with an electric car, and planned accordingly. But for "Joe Public" there is an expectation that using an electric car will be as easy as fueling an ICE car, and in most people's minds that equates to a ubiquitous charging infrastructure and charging from empty to full in a matter of minutes.[18]

---

[18] The website Plug In America (http://pluginamerica.org) is a great resource for general info on electric cars, road trips and charging. Also check out their regular EV podcast series (http://www.pluginamerica.org/ev-media/podcasts)

While I don't believe that either of these things are necessary for the vast majority of owners—largely due to being able to charge at home and relatively short average journeys—the perception still exists.

> Range anxiety and the lack of a ubiquitous charging infrastructure have been the major barriers to the mainstream adoption of battery electric vehicles.

Elon Musk and the executive team at Tesla have systematically set out to demolish every barrier to mainstream adoption. 70 mile range not good enough? How about 300! Not sporty enough? How's 0 to 60 in 3 seconds? Worried about lack of charging stations? No problem! We'll build a global charging infrastructure and make it free to use. Er, what?

Tesla Supercharger, Fort Myers, FL.

Yes. You read it correctly. Tesla is building a global network of charging stations—called *Superchargers*—for Model S (and subsequent cars). And they are free to use. And they will be powered by sunlight. Imagine travelling anywhere in North America or Europe, stopping every now and again for a 15-20 minutes for a quick boost and not paying one cent. And no smelly, flammable fuel splashing on your feet!

Jump to Chapter 19 to learn more about Superchargers and how they work, including "sunlight power."

4 Range and Performance

Introduction

In the first part of the book you got a brief introduction to Model S, and now it's time to get into the nitty-gritty. Model S is unlike any other car that has traveled the world's roads. And because it's different, the first thing that every potential Model S customer must do is to evaluate whether this revolutionary vehicle is a good personal choice.

Invariably, the very first issue that comes to mind is *range anxiety*—the worry about how far a Model S can go before you have to charge it. For old technology vehicles (i.e., vehicles with gasoline or diesel powered internal combustion engines), you don't worry about range because an extensive refill infrastructure (gas stations) has evolved over the past 100 years. When an ICE vehicle runs low on fuel, you stop at a nearby gas station and fill it. Model S and EVs in general are exactly the same, but the refill infrastructure for EVs is not yet as robust, so running low of charge worries potential buyers.

What many potential owners forget is that unlike ICE cars—where we *have* to go to the gas station to refill, with a BEV you can refuel at home. Plug in at night and *the car is full every morning*. Many Model S owners have *never* had to recharge away from home. But what if you do want to go a really long way?

Range Anxiety—Should I be Worried?

As I already mentioned, it's the first question on everyone's mind. But honestly, it shouldn't be. At the time of this writing, Tesla Superchargers allow you to drive the Model S (at zero fuel cost) from Miami to New York to Los Angeles. Just as important, the network is expanding very rapidly throughout North America and Europe.

In addition, the public charging infrastructure is growing quickly. In 2011 (long before Tesla's Supercharger network began) there were 1,972 charging stations in the U.S., but by May, 2013, the number had exploded to 20,138.[19] The Tesla supercharging network is growing rapidly with hundreds of stations in operation in the United States. To get a real-time feel for the current network, visit: http://www.teslamotors.com/supercharger

---

[19] http://www.fool.com/investing/general/2014/01/24/what-will-it-take-to-get-americans-buying-electric.aspx

THE SUPERCHARGER SOLUTION

I discussed the Supercharger network briefly in Chapter 3. Almost every Model S owner will make an occasional trip of 250 miles or more. If you travel along or near interstates, a quick stop at a Supercharger will enable you to extend the range of Model S to whatever distance you need.

> Model S can be charged at a Tesla Supercharger at no cost. In 20 minutes, you'll be able to get up to 150 miles of range added to your battery.

Every stop does require 15-30 minutes of your time, but then again, if you were told that you could get a free tank of gas if you'd wait 20 minutes, instead of the typical 5-10 minutes at a gas station, would you do it? That's the bargain that the Supercharger option provides for Model S owners.

FOR DRIVERS WHO TRAVEL NO MORE THAN 100 MILES PER DAY

If normal driving takes you no more than 100 miles in a day, there is really no need to worry about range. Every Model S, including the (now discontinued) 60 kWh model[20], provides a sufficient range buffer for your driving patterns and can easily accommodate round trips of 100 miles or less, even at typical highway speeds of 75+ mph. Just plug Model S into your home outlet and your car is "full" every morning. At 100 miles there is sufficient buffer to cope with anything that temperature, wind or elevation changes might throw at you. Range anxiety disappears.

FOR DRIVERS WHO TRAVEL BETWEEN 100 AND 150 MILES PER DAY

A Certified Pre-Owned 60 kWh model may work for you, but with the 85 kWh battery or even the new 70 kWh models you'll rarely have to think about charging on the go.[21]

FOR DRIVERS WHO TRAVEL BETWEEN 150 AND 220 MILES PER DAY

If you drive moderately, don't have significant elevation changes on your route (e.g., you don't regularly travel through mountainous areas), and travel the majority of your distance on an interstate, Model S will work for you. You'll

---

[20] Replaced by the 70 kWh model in April 2015.
[21] If you drive more conservatively, range increases significantly and you'll easily be able to take daily round trips of 210-220 miles.

probably need an 85kWh battery for peace of mind (but the 70 kWh might be enough), and you might consider the High Power Home Charging option (twin chargers and the High Power Wall Connector) in case you need a quick fill up at home. Your decision becomes simple if you have a Supercharger along your route or have charging facilities at your regular destination, but overall, Model S is viable transportation in this range.

FOR DRIVERS WHO REGULARY TRAVEL VERY LONG DISTANCES

If you're a driver who regularly travels very long distances—250 miles or more per round trip[22]—the decision is a bit more complex. If your travels take you on a route that passes a Supercharger *and* you can afford the small amount of time required to gain a half charge (20 minutes), there's really no significant concern about range. If your round trip includes several hours at one location (e.g., to a place of work) that has charging capability you may still be OK. But if your travels take you on routes that do not currently have the Supercharger infrastructure in place, it may be that you'll have to wait until battery technologies improve to the 400–500 mile range before you buy a battery electric vehicle like Model S or its successors.[23]

What Affects Range the Most? _____

As I noted earlier in this chapter, range (rightly or wrongly) continues to be an issue when BEVs are considered. Even though Model S has substantial range, driving long distances requires some planning. In this section we'll consider the technical aspects of range and range planning.

This is where it gets a little complicated, but no more complicated than a gasoline car (and in some ways simpler).

Important: If you want to skip this section you can assume that Joe Average driver will get about 200–220 miles from an 85 kWh battery, , 170–200 miles from a 70 kWh battery and 140–150 from a 60kWh battery. Really cold weather can use 30% more battery, and air conditioning can use 10% more.

---

[22] Distances in this range, traveled on a regular basis, mean that you are one of a very small (considerably less than 1 percent) of drivers who do ultra-long commutes or who drive long distances as part of their work.
[23] At the time of writing there is no commitment from Tesla Motors to produce such a battery for Model S or Model X.

For any car, range is a function of how much energy the car can store (i.e., gas in the gas tank, charge in the batteries) and how much energy it uses (miles per gallon, Watt-hours per mile.[24])

To obtain the maximum driving range for any vehicle, the designers want to maximize available energy and minimize energy use. There are two ways to maximize available energy: (1) design a large fuel tank or a big battery and/or (2) use fuels with a high *energy density*.

In a similar manner, there are a number of ways to minimize energy use. The biggest consumers of energy in a car are:

- Inefficiencies in the engine (motor) and drivetrain
- Rolling resistance (moving the tires over the road surface)
- Aerodynamic drag (moving the air out of the way, especially at speed)
- Air conditioning and other components

In addition, the environment also consumes (or gives back) energy:

- Head winds and tail winds
- Going up or down hills
- Heat and cold

In the following pages we'll explore each of these items in some detail.

AVAILABLE ENERGY

Gasoline has a high "energy density'—in other words you can pack a lot of "oomph" into a pretty small space (or a pretty low weight). Lithium-ion batteries like those in Model S (and most BEVs) have a much lower energy density. Per unit of volume, gasoline has between 20 and 30 times the "oomph" compared to Lithium-ion cells.[25] It is possible to use exotic battery chemistry to increase the "oomph," but that would be prohibitably expensive, and possibly dangerous. Currently, Lithium-ion gives the best "oomph per dollar" for BEVs.

We therefore want as big a battery as possible to compensate for this low energy density. Of course, there are always design trade-offs. The bigger the

---

[24] See the Glossary for an explanation of Wh/m
[25] For the more technical reader, gasoline has an energy density of c. 36 MJ/L, whereas Lithium-ion batteries are 1-2 MJ/L

battery, the heavier the vehicle. And the higher the weight, the more energy is required to propel the vehicle forward. The key is to optimize—achieving the biggest battery while keeping the weight of the car under control. Tesla has therefore gone to great lengths to minimize the weight of Model S while maximizing the battery capacity.

Model S has the biggest battery of any production BEV: 70kWh, 85kWh or 90kWh, depending on the model. By comparison, the Nissan Leaf uses a 24kWh battery, The Chevrolet Volt 16.5 kWh, and the Mitsubshi i-MiEV only 16kWh.[26]

> *To summarize:* Getting long range from a battery-powered car requires that it (a) has a lot of batteries, (b) uses very little energy, or (c) both.

CONSUMERS OF ENERGY

Converting the fuel in the tank to speed on the highway incurs many energy losses in addition to the energy needed to move the car forwards. Aerodynamic drag, rolling resistance, road friction, and mechanical friction affect Model S as they would an ICE car. But where the BEV wins out is in the conversion of energy in the fuel to forward motion.

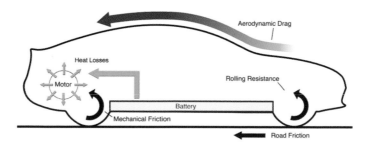

Some losses, such as rolling resistance, are not materially affected by speed.[27] Others, especially aerodynamic drag, vary dramatically with speed. Motor efficiency also varies with speed (motor RPM). The graph below shows how the various elements make up the total energy use in Model S at different speeds. As you can see, rolling resistance accounts for the majority of the energy use up to about 60 mph, and then aerodynamic drag begins to dominate.

---

[26] See the Glossary for an explanation of kWh
[27] Although rolling resistance does go down by approximately one third after about 20-30 minutes as tires warm up.

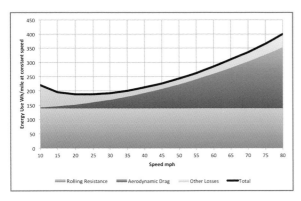

I've researched what the "other losses" might be. My understanding is that they are primarily heat loss from the powertrain, combined with motor and inverter inefficiency. Energy use by the accessories and other friction losses are relatively small.

If we were to assume that ALL of the energy loss in the green part of the chart is due to the motor's inefficiency in converting electricity from the

battery into forward motion (which it isn't but let's assume worst case), then we can calculate an efficiency curve for the powertrain:

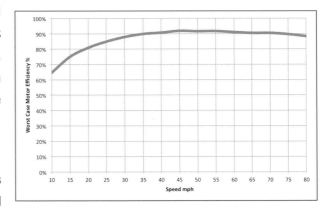

Remember that this is worst case. The actual motor efficiency is probably better than this. You can see from the graph that Model S powertrain efficiency ranges from 65–93% and is over 90% for a large part of the rev range (80 mph is nearly 10,000 rpm). Gas and Diesel cars are typically around *30–35% efficient*, and even the best are in the low 40's!

> The Model S powertrain is *at least twice, and in some cases three times* more efficient than the powertrain in internal combustion engine cars.

Tesla has also managed something remarkable for its all-wheel drive 'D' variants of Model S. Typically, all-wheel drive systems reduce range due to addition weight and higher friction losses in the drive train.

> With its unique dual motor approach, using different reduction gears in the two motors, Tesla has been able to *increase* the range of the all-wheel drive variants compared to the rear-wheel drive equivalents.

Real World Range_____

Real world range is very much a function of how you drive, and the environment in which you drive (wind, temperature, and elevation changes). To understand what your range is likely to be, you'll need to assess your driving habits honestly.

Like ICE cars, Model S energy use (fuel consumption) varies quite significantly with speed. If you take motor efficiency into account, then the actual consumption measured at the battery looks like this:

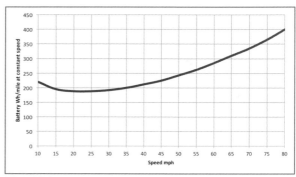

Model S fuel consumption versus speed.

> The number one factor that affects range is speed. Model S will go roughly *half as far* at 80 mph as it will at 40 mph.

It is clear from the fuel consumption vs. speed graph that Model S is most economical at 20-25 mph, and that fuel consumption rises quickly as the speed increases. What *isn't* obvious is just how economical Model S is. Most people who are familar with Model S would probably say that it is more economical than a typical sedan, and certainly more economic than an SUV—even the hybrid SUVs that are appearing on the market. But what about a Toyota Prius? Model S fuel consumption is about the same as a Prius? Right?

Wrong. Model S is not only *much* more fuel-efficient than a typical ICE car, it is *much* more fuel-efficient than a Toyota Prius. The chart that follows shows fuel consumption

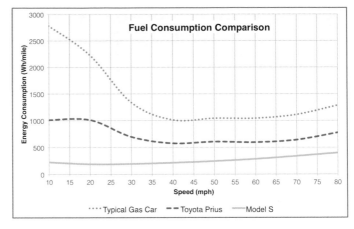

versus speed for a typical ICE car, the Toyota Prius and Model S.

As you can see, Model S typically uses significantly less energy than hybrids or ICE cars. One other thing to note is that Model S is most efficient at about 25 mph, whereas an ICE car is typically most efficient at 40-60 mph. One consequence of this is that if you do run into range problems, slowing down will help you get to where you need to be.

Any discussion of real world range is complicated by many factors you can't control and one really important one that you can—your personal driving habits. Drive the car hard (80 mph[28] on the interstate), and your range will suffer. Drive it more calmly, and you'll get advertised range and more.

ENERGY USE: ACCELERATION

There's a complementary question that many Model S owners ask: Does hard acceleration have a significant impact on range? Unless you are trying to be a Formula 1 driver, the answer is "not really." The efficency map for the motor is relatively flat across the rev and power range. Accelerating hard will use more energy, but not that much.

> The amazing efficiency of the electric motor means that driving at 70 vs 50 has a MUCH bigger impact on range than accelerating from 0-60 in 4 seconds vs 8 seconds.

---

[28] Obviously only do this where the local traffic regulations allow you to.

ENERGY USE: ROOF RACKS AND TOWING

Earlier in the book, I mentioned that Model S has a slippery drag coefficient, remarkably good for a production vehicle. Anything that increases the drag coefficient negatively impacts the range and performance of the car.

In general, any add-on that protrudes from the existing surface of Model S will increase drag. Roof racks protrude, so roof racks are to be avoided if at all possible. Tesla has made a roof rack available in the online store (you'll need a panoramic roof to use it) but avoid it if you can, and certainly don't leave it installed when not in use unless you want to see your energy use go up considerably.

Model S does not have a tow hitch, primarily because of the negative impact towing has on range.

Forum user **@Pungoteague_Dave** fitted the EcoHitch from TorkLift Central and drove from the US North East down to Florida and back (2410 miles) and reported[29] a paltry 5 Wh/m impact. This contrasts sharply with his experience with a bike rack and two bikes on the back, which increased his consumption by 125 Wh/m at 60 mph! As always, "your mileage may vary." (See the *Customizing* Chapter for more information on aftermarket tow hitch solutions if you really, really must tow something.)

> If you absolutely, positively insist on using a "factory" roof rack, you MUST have the panoramic roof because it includes cutouts in the roof rails.[30]

ENERGY USE: HOT AND COLD CLIMATES

Many Model S owners live in moderate climates, where heating or air conditioning are not significant issues. However, for those Model S owners who live in extreme climates (either hot or cold), energy drain due to heating or cooling does need to be considered.

> Overall, moderate cabin heating and cooling doesn't have too big an impact on range—no more than 10% of total energy use. But cold weather (below 40°F) can have up to a 30% negative impact on range.

[29] http://www.teslamotors.com/forum/forums/2410mile-trailertowing-trip-virginia-palm-beach-back-added-pictures
[30] It's worth noting that Model S has voluminous interior storage, so it may be possible to get along without a roof rack.

In cold climates:

- Using heated seats is MUCH more efficient than heating the entire cabin. So if range is a concern, turn the temperature down in the cabin, and use the seat heaters. You'll save energy and improve the range of your Model S.

- Cold air is more dense and as a consequence, drag increases slightly. More importantly, Model S will heat the battery to an optimal temperature, which consumes a fair amount of energy. The result is that your range will be lower.

Handling in Snow: **Many people are concerned about how electric cars perform and handle in low temperatures and snow. Will it work? Is the rear wheel drive enough? In short, yes. Check out this 300km trip in the snow in Norway for detailed answers to these and other questions: http://youtu.be/XZ5PqPeOPTO**

In hot climates:

- Hot weather demands A/C, but because hot air is less dense, drag is reduced. If it is hot enough to require A/C, then A/C use is likely to have only a 5% negative impact on range (but could be as high as 10%).

- High TSER (Total Solar Energy Rejection) window film will reduce the solar heat going into the car. As a consequence, it will reduce your need for A/C and reduce the impact on range.

Many potential Model S owners in hot climates worry about heating that will occur as a consequence of the panoramic roof option. They often ask whether they'll need a shade on the panoramic roof or some other mechanism (e.g., film) for cutting heat transmission through the roof.

Heat and the Panoramic Roof: **Tesla has implemented an excellent heat resistant roof material that incorporates films to cut heat transfer by as much as 81 percent. As a consequence, very little heat is transmitted through the panoramic roof. You need not worry about cabin over-heating when you order the panoramic roof option.**

ENERGY USE: HILLS

Going uphill is remarkably energy intensive. Gaining 5000 ft. of elevation in Model S takes the same amount of energy as driving *30 miles at 60 mph*! The good thing is that, unlike an ICE car, Model S gains most of that energy back (about 80%) when you come down!

The reason for that energy gain is, of course, *regenerative braking—* something that you've already learned about.

> **When going down a hill, Model S gains back up to 80% of the energy it took to get up the hill—if you use regeneration.**

One aspect of elevation that isn't often discussed is the *dramatic decrease* in performance that ICE cars suffer at high elevation due to the thinner atmosphere. Normally aspirated gas cars typically lose 3-4% of power for every 1000 ft. of elevation. So a 300-horsepower Porsche will deliver closer to 200 horsepower if you are high in the Rocky Mountains! With Model S there is *no decrease* in performance with altitude.

ENERGY USE: WIND

We've discussed in some detail the impact of aerodynamic drag on range. One thing that many drivers don't appreciate is the impact of wind. It's simple physics—driving at 40 mph into a 40 mph headwind is equivalent to driving at 80 mph—so expect your range to halve. But the opposite is also true: drive 40 mph with a 40 mph tail wind and expect your range to increase by about 30%!

ENERGY USE: ALL-WHEEL DRIVE

The dual-motor variants of Model S have all-wheel drive. In an ICE car, all-wheel drive will almost certainly increase fuel consumption due to the additional weight and friction losses of the more complex drive train. Through clever engineering and design choices Tesla has managed to not only eliminate this efficiency penalty for the all-wheel drive Model S, but the S85D variant of the car is actually more efficient, and has a longer range, than the rear-wheel drive S85. Electric motors can be virtually frictionless when not in use, and Tesla uses "torque sleep"—tuning the motor electronics to eliminate any magnetic drag when not in use—to accomplish this. Additionally, drive electronics switch power to either or both of the motors as appropriate on a millisecond-to-millisecond basis to optimize the efficiency.

Performance specs—what's real/what's not? _____

When some consumers think of BEVs they envision tiny econo-boxes whose performance is—well—less than good. Things change radically when you evaluate Model S. Prepare to be impressed.

REAL-WORLD SUMMARY:

- Top speed: 130-155 mph
- Acceleration: 0-60 in 5.9[31] to 2.8[32] seconds

Let's explore the details behind these numbers, starting with the easy ones first.

TOP SPEED

Model S is electronically limited to 140 mph (70, 70D, S85) or 155 mph (S85D, P85D). Unlike stick-shift (manual) or automatic transmission cars that have between three and eight gears, Model S uses a single gear with a 9.73:1 reduction ratio[33] that connects the motor to the differential. It requires no clutch or torque-converter.

> Because Model S does not have a complex transmission, between 800 and 1000 parts that would add weight, reduce range, and require maintenance are eliminated. Compared to an ICE or hybrid car, there's much less that can go wrong in the Model S drivetrain.

The electric motor revs to about 16,000 rpm, so a quick bit of math based on the tire diameter will show that the motor hits max revs at about the point where the limiter kicks in.

---

[31] 60 kWh model
[32] Performance 85/90 Dual-motor model with "Ludicrous Mode".
[33] It is believed that the dual-motor variants use a different reduction ratio on the front motor, but this has not been confirmed by Tesla.

ACCELERATION

Model S is "crazy quick" when it comes to acceleration. The S70 is the slowest Model S to 60 mph, taking a leisurely 5.5 seconds. To put that in context, 5.5 seconds is 2 seconds *faster* than the Ferrari 308 Tom Selleck drove in *Magnum, P.I.* and is faster than a 1989 Ferrari Testarossa.

> There's a phenomenon that is well known to Model S owners. It's called the "Tesla Grin." You'll see it every time you take a friend for a test drive and you nail the accelerator (and believe me, you'll be asked for test drives).

The G forces are so profound and the acceleration is so pronounced and fluid that your guest can do only one thing—grin. After the grin there is usually an intake of breath, followed by a comment like "holy #$%&#!"

The P90D, at 2.8 seconds, has pretty much the same 0 to 60 and ¼ mile times as the $1 million McLaren F1.

In real-world conditions many owners have found that Model S (especially the P85D) will out accelerate pretty much everything. The 0 to 60 times published for most ICE cars are the best possible times taken from a selection of runs by professional drivers in ideal conditions with every possible combination of launch control enabled, and with the high likelihood of destroying the clutch due to the violent nature of the high-rev starts. Conversely, Model S published times are accessible to "Joe Average" driver under typical road conditions. Stated simply, the car is wicked fast!

The incredible acceleration of Model S is a combination of many design elements, but is fundamentally due to the differences in behavior between gasoline or diesel engines and electric motors. The ability of a car to accelerate is predominently governed by three factors:

- the torque produced by the motor
- the weight of the car, and
- the adhesion of the tires.

Unless you start stripping the car down and throwing things out, the weight is out of your control. So for a given combination of tires and road surface the number one factor for acceleration is torque. Torque (not power) is the thing that pushes the car forward.

[An aside: people often focus on the "power" of the engine. Engines (and motors) produce torque, and power is simply a measure of torque times engine speed. Torque generally decreases with high rpm, therefore a "high power" engine is one in which there is still reasonable torque at high revs.]

Torque in a gas engine is largely dependent on the size and number of explosions that are happening in the combustion chambers. If the engine isn't turning, no explosions are happening, so there is zero torque. In Model S, motor torque is dependent on the magnetic fields generated by the electric current. Even if the motor isn't turning, a massive magnetic field can be created. This leads to a strange (compared to a gas engine) phoenomenon that *maximum torque is obtained at zero rpm*. There is no need to wait for the engine to "get up to speed". This is what gives Model S its amazing acceleration, and is the source of the *Tesla Grin*.

Comparing the torque curve of Model S P85 to that of a Porsche 911 Carrera[34] we see a number of significant differences:

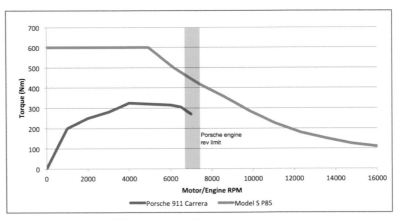

Torque curve Model S P85 vs. Porsche 911 Carrera

1. Model S produces *much* more torque than the Porsche, especially at low revs.
2. The operating rev range of the Porsche engine is much smaller (7000 rpm) than Model S (16,000 rpm). The high rpm limit of Model S combined with the high torque eliminates the need for a multiple gears.

---

[34] This graph represents public domain data from one dynamometer reading and may not be representative of the many different variants of Porsche's 911 cars.

3. Model S produces maximum torque from 0-5000 rpm. There is no need to rev the engine, nor engage "launch control" or other electronic trickery to produce fast, clean acceleration.

4. The Porsche curve has a peak that is not very wide—meaning that the car needs to be held between 3500-6500 rpm to get maximum performance, and needs to frequently change gear when accelerating.

> Electric motors produce maximum torque at zero revs. It is a simple matter of pressing on the accelerator to extract the maximum "oomph."

Combine this with the virtually instantaneous delivery of electrons and the direct connection of the motor to the rear axle, versus the complex process of squirting and vaporizing precise amounts of gasoline, taking up the slack in the various complex joints between the pistons, crank shaft, thrust bearing, clutch plates, universal joints and drive shafts, and you have acceleration like the Starship Enterprise.

5 Configuring and Ordering

It's time to design your Model S. Head on over to the Tesla website and start checking some boxes. Unfortunately, like thousands of Model S buyers before you, as soon as you start to configure your car you'll almost certainly be confronted by a whole host of questions to which you have few answers. In this chapter I'll try and give you some guidance for the most common decisions a Model S buyer must make.

Current model line up

We are now three years into Model S production and a number of models have been introduced, and others discontinued. We'll start out with the list of new cars available at the time of writing:

Model[35]	Rated Range[36] (miles)	Power (hp) (front/rear)	0-60 (sec)	1/4 mile (sec)	Top Speed (mph)	Auto-pilot-capable	Introduced
S70	230	315 (382)[37]	5.5	13.8	140	Yes	Jul 2015
S70D	240	328 (259/259)[37]	5.2	13.5	140	Yes	Apr 2015
S85 v2[34]	265	373	5.4	13.5	140	Yes	Oct 2014
S85D[38]	270	417[39] (259/259)[37]	4.2	12.5	155	Yes	Oct 2014
P85D	253	761 (259/503)[37]	3.1[40]	11.7	155	Yes	Oct 2014
S90	TBD[41]	373	5.4	13.5	140	Yes	Jul 2015
S90D	TBD	417 (259/259)[37]	4.2	11.7	155	Yes	Jul 2015
P90D	TBD	761 (259/503)[37]	2.8[40]	10.9	155	Yes	Jul 2015

All cars have exactly the same body style and color choices, and virtually the same trim options and feature choices (see the following pages for details).

---

[35] Although I've designated version 1 and version 2 models, the cars have been constantly tweaked since their first introduction with new hardware and software features added and removed on a frequent basis. Version 2 represents a significant change with the addition of autopilot and optional dual motors.
[36] Rated Range measurements shown here are based on EPA 5-cycle tests.
[37] Maximum available motor power
[38] 'D' variants are all wheel drive with one motor driving the front wheels, and another driving the rear; non-'D' variants are rear wheel drive.
[39] When 85D was introduced power was rated at 376 hp total, 188 hp front and 188 hp rear
[40] In July 2015 the 'Ludicrous Speed' option was introduced which decreases the 0-60 time to 2.8 seconds, standing quarter to 10.9 and reduces the 0-155 mph time by 20%.
[41] EPA ranges for 90 kWh batteries were not available at the time of publication

Discontinued models

Tesla has been evolving the Model S continuously over the last three years, and as new variants were introduced others were discontinued. Used cars (including models that are now discontinued) are appearing as current owners trade up. To help you with your purchase decision, below you'll find the list of discontinued Model S variants. Although they are no longer available new directly from Tesla, these are still some of the most amazing cars on the market.

Model[42]	Rated Range[43] (miles)	Power (hp) (front/rear)	0-60 (sec)	Top Speed (mph)	Auto-pilot-capable	Introduced	Discontinued
S40 v1[44]	132	235	6.5	110	No	Jun 2012	Apr 2013[45]
S60 v1	208	302	5.6	120	No	Jun 2012	Oct 2014
S85 v1	265	362	5.2	125	No	Jun 2012	Oct 2014
P85 v1	265	416	4.2	130	No	Jun 2012	Oct 2014
P85+	265	416	4.2	130	No[46]	May 2013	Nov 2014
S60D[47]	208	376 (188/188)	5.7	125	Yes	Oct 2014	Nov 2014
P85 v2	265	470	4.2	155	Yes	Oct 2014	Nov 2014
S60 v2	208	380	5.9	120	Yes	Oct 2014	Apr 2015

---

[42] Although I've designated version 1 and version 2 models, the cars have been constantly tweaked since their first introduction with new hardware and software features added and removed on a frequent basis. Version 2 represents a significant change with the addition of autopilot and optional dual motors.
[43] Rated Range measurements shown here are based on EPA 5-cycle tests.
[44] The S40 had a 60 kWh battery that was software restricted to 40 kWh
[45] The S40 was the first car to be discontinued, due to low sales (and very high demand for the other models). S40 owners were offered the option to eliminate the software restriction on the battery pack.
[46] A very small number of cars built during September and October 2014 had driver assist hardware.
[47] The S60D and new P85 were removed from the model line up only a month after being offered for sale to simplify the production process and thereby reduce costs. The P85+ was also removed.

First question: which model? 70, 70D, 85, 85D or P85D?____

70: The 70 kWh Tesla Model S (70) is the least expensive Model S variant. Its range is remarkably good, and it can be tricked out with almost every interior and exterior option available for the more costly variants.

70D: The 70 kWh Tesla Model S Dual Motor Version (70D) is (in my opinion) the best value Model S variant. It has better range than the S70, and like its sibling can be tricked out with almost every interior and exterior option available for the more costly variants. With all-wheel drive as standard, the 70D has become the default choice for many owners.

85: The 85 kWh Tesla Model S (85) is the next step up. The larger battery increases the range by 10% and improves acceleration slightly. This car was the 'default' option for most owners before the 70D was introduced.

85D: The 85 kWh Tesla Model S Dual Motor Version (85D), introduced in October 2014 brought all wheel drive to the lineup. With a 0-60 time almost as good as the original Performance 85, it yields the longest range of the four models.

P85D: Topping out the model range is the 85 kWh Tesla Model S Performance Dual Motor Version (P85D). It is difficult to avoid superlatives with this car. With all wheel drive, 761 peak horsepower[48], over 900 lb.ft of torque, and a 0-60 time of 2.8 seconds this is truly a supercar. One of the on-screen settings is "Ludicrous Mode" ! Yet it seats five (or seven) and has incredible fuel economy. There is nothing like it on the road.

See the **Range Upgrade** section later in this chapter for information about the 90 kWh variants.

---

[48] With the $10,000 'Ludicrous' option – yes, it really is called that.

Options—worth it or not?

Which model you choose is often dependent on what you can afford, and this sometimes means a trade off between the model and the options. Do I go with the biggest battery but forego the tech package and panoramic roof? Is a sub-three-second 0-60 time worth the extra money? Let's explore the available options and some of the potential trade-offs.

Model S comes with an assortment of options that range from aesthetic enhancements to functional capabilities. All improve your Model S experience in some manner. But they're options for a reason. Not everyone wants a high-end audio system or a panoramic roof, or other small aesthetic tweaks. For that reason, personal taste and the need for specific functions and features will dictate your choices.

> The Tesla Motors website has an excellent online configurator[49] that explains all the options, the different possible combinations and their prices.

Let's spend a little time going through the less obvious aspects of some of the options and, in an effort to help you make an informed choice, examine their pros and cons. I'll make a "buy it" or "maybe" recommendation where appropriate, but I recognize that everyone's tastes and needs are different.

Car Color

Color is a very personal decision and your choice depends on aesthetics, the amount of work you want to do to keep your Model S clean (certain colors show less dirt), the color of your friend's Model S (you'll probably want something different), and a variety of other factors (e.g., the opinion of your significant other!)

---

[49] http://www.teslamotors.com/models/design

Model S comes in a small range of colors arranged in three color-categories:

Basic (Black and White)

Metallic (Titanium, Midnight Silver, Obsidian Black, and Deep Blue)

Multi-coat (Pearl-white and Red)

After much deliberation I went with Pearl-white—and I absolutely love it! It also seems to be the favorite color of most of the Tesla employees I've spoken to, though Multi-coat Red seems to be the most popular color amongst owners.

If none of these colors take your fancy, with today's high quality vinyl wraps it's possible to pick from hundreds of possible colors—if you're willing to spend the money on an aftermarket solution. Check out the section on "wrapping" in Chapter 17 for some examples of what Model S owners have done.

And if money is really no object, you may be able to get a factory custom paint job in a translucent pinkish hue (as one owner actually did!).[50]

Originally it was possible to order a black roof with any colored car, but this option was discontinued in 2014.

Interior Upholstery and Trim Options

The interior of Model S is one of the more controversial areas of the car. Some owners have argued that it is too sparse, while others say that the minimalist look is just what they desire. Many owners have suggested that the lack of "grab-handles" above the doors is a serious omission, that a lack of built-in rear coat hangers and rear cup holders is a problem[51], and that interior lighting and amenities need improvement. Most of these issues represent personal style preferences and do not impact the driving experience significantly (though my wife and children disagree).

The interior trim combinations have changed significantly over the first thirty months of the car's production. Initially only available in Nappa leather, textile seats were added in mid-2013. The Alcantara headliner was originally bundled with the performance leather seats but then offered as a separate option, as was the extended Nappa leather trim. Black Alcantara was added as an alternative to the white (actually more like tan) Alcantara.

The wood veneers that Tesla has chosen are somewhat unusual by auto industry standards. There are no burled wood grains, nor any light colors. All wood veneers fall into the brown/black color palette.

 **Lacewood** (now discontinued) was available during 2012-2013 and is the most unusual of the wood veneers, providing an open grain look and more texture than any of the other trims finishes. The open "plates" in the Lacewood

---

[50] Custom colors were available for a short period when Model S was first offered for sale in the US.
[51] Elon chose not to put coat hangers in for aesthetic reasons. Originally he didn't plan to put reading lights in the second row either, but changed his mind after his son said their absence made Model S the "stupidest car in the world." http://www.lawac.org/speech-archive/pdf/1659.pdf

provide a unique look that distinguishes this veneer from the others.

 **Obeche wood** has a strong horizontal grain (vertical in early cars) that is offered in both matte and high gloss finishes. Obeche wood works surprisingly well in Model S. The Obeche matte finish is subdued and has a dark brown look. The gloss finish causes the grain to "pop" and looks more brown than the matte.

Piano black is high gloss black—beautiful, but likely to show every fingerprint. It gives the interior a clean, modern feel and works well with every upholstery choice.

Finally, **carbon fiber** provides a very cool high tech look that is quite popular.

Each store has a display showing trim colors and materials.

Based on actual market data from my friends at evannex,com, the most popular trims are Carbon Fiber, Obeche Gloss, and Obeche Matte in that order. Piano Black is considerably less common.

Here are the decisions you'll have to make as you design the interior décor for your Model S. This is very much an aesthetic choice, but for what it's worth I chose carbon fiber along with my tan interior.

Q. Do I want Textile or Nappa Leather?

Some buyers are philosophically opposed to the use of leather and choose textile as a matter of conscience. I respect that. Others argue that textile is cooler in hot weather and less "sticky" in feel. But Model S is a premium car, and the vast majority of buyers choose Nappa leather to provide a richer, more luxurious interior. Note that Model S has (at the time of writing) heated—but not cooled—seats. My tan leather seats do not generally become hot here in the sun in South Florida. Although, to be fair, I do have tinted windows.

At the time of writing there is a $1500 price difference between textile and Nappa leather seats.

Q. If I chose leather upholstery, what interior color is appropriate?

This decision, like all aesthetic decisions, is personal. Most buyers want the interior leather color and the exterior paint color to complement one another.

Black interiors work with all light paint colors and provide a modern feel. They are the most stain and dirt resistant.

Tan upholstery works well with every paint color and provides a beautiful look regardless of the trim choices you make.

Grey leather is a nice choice for dark paint colors and works very well with Carbon Fiber, Lacewood, and Piano Black.

Signature cars in the US had the choice of white leather—not something I'd personally risk.

Leather it is. Do I need 'next generation' seats or should I go with standard?

Initially available only on the P85D, "next generation" seats provide much larger bolsters for additional lateral support, and generally feel more luxurious than the standard seats. They were created in response to criticism from owners that the standard seats were not on par with those from Audi, BMW, Mercedes or Porsche.

Regular (left) versus Next Generation (right) seats. Photo © Tesla Motors.

Next generation seats are (at the time of writing) a $2,000 upgrade from standard leather seats.

Prior to October 2014 Tesla offered "performance" seats. These were standard leather seats with Alcantara inserts and colored piping.

In very early cars, standard seats had fewer adjustments and the 'standard' versus "performance" was more meaningful. The specification was updated so that both types of seat became 12-way adjustable.

Both driver and front passenger seats are 12-way adjustable, but only the driver's seat position is stored in the driver profile memory (see below)

Q. Should I order the Premium Interior Package?

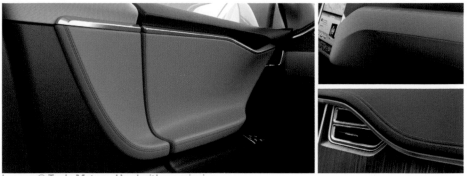

Images © Tesla Motors. Used with permission

Tesla bundled together a number of separate options to create the premium interior package. These are "extended Nappa leather trim" (this option covers the dash, instrument panel, door panels, console, and driver airbag cover in leather to complement the seats), "interior accent lighting" (LEDs positioned throughout the interior to subtly light the car), and the "décor matched yacht floor" (the floor of the center console space). I like the look and think it adds even more style, but it is expensive and would be an easy option to drop if you are looking to save money.

Q. Which headliner should I choose?

The Alcantara headliner is another great place to save money. I have it because it came standard with the P85, but I don't think I'd miss it if it weren't there. White versus black headliner is very much a personal choice.

Wheels—21-inch vs. 19-inch

In my opinion, a car's wheels are one of the most important elements that define the car's look. Model S provides a variety of wheel choices, ranging from practical, but somewhat stodgy, 19-inch five-spoke rims to the spectacular 21-inch Turbine wheels in silver and grey (originally available on the P85 and P85+ only, now an open option).

For Model S owners who live in cold climates or in cities with lots of potholes, the 19-inch, five-spoke wheels are an excellent and practical choice. But if you want automotive bling, the 21's are your choice. Sure, they're a bit impractical. Yes, the tires wear more rapidly. And yeah, one bad pothole could wreck the rim. But they look really great and are, in my opinion, the designer's choice for the car. Many cold-climate owners run 21's in the summer, and have a set of 19's with winter tires.

Last but not least are the 19-inch Cyclones, added late in 2013 in response to owner demands for a 19-inch equivalent to the Turbine wheels. I think they look better in real life than in the design studio, and are a great alternative to the 21-inch Turbines at $2,000 less.

For a period during 2013 it was possible to configure 19-inch "Aero" wheels that added 3% range. These are now available only in the online store as part of the "Winter Wheel" package. The optional Michelin Primacy tires provide a similar range improvement and can be configured with the initial order.

19" Standard Wheels

19" Aero Wheels

19" Cyclone Wheels

21" Turbine Wheels

21" Grey Turbine Wheels

By all accounts the 19's are slightly quieter, while the 21's have more traction. The 21's decrease range by between 3–6% due to higher rolling resistance.

The 21-inch Turbine wheels are NOT cheap, and many owners opt for the 19's and upgrade with aftermarket 20's, 21's or even 22's. See Chapter 17, Customizing and Accessorizing, for some examples.

Autopilot

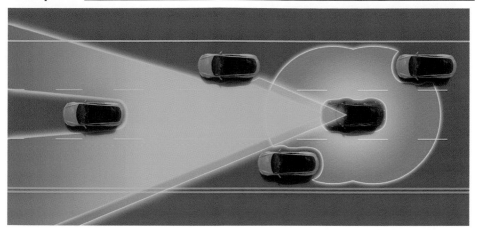

Driver assist capabilities were added to the Model S options list following the opening of the new factory production line in August 2014. New hardware includes a forward looking camera, radar and 360-degree ultransonic sensors. Features are gradually being enabled via software upgrades; the first two are speed-limit assist and lane-change warnings. These supplement the park distance sensors (park assist) that was already available.

Current features include adaptive cruise control, and automatic high/low beam headlights. In the future Tesla will enable, via free software updates, additional capabilities such as automatic lane change and self steering, leading to full 'autopilot' (the ability of the car to drive 90% of a journey with no driver input).

Though the hardware is installed as standard, it has to be software enabled for $2500 at time of purchase, or $3000 after purchase. It is definitely worth having.

The Tech Package

The Tech Package was a mainstay of the car throughout the first two and a half years from the launch, though contents varied considerably over time. In July 2015 Tesla removed the Tech Package and moved virtually everything into the base car configuration, which now includes:

> "Free long distance travel on the Supercharger network; Maps and navigation with real time traffic updates; 8 year, infinite mile battery and drive unit warranty; Automatic

keyless entry; Daytime running lights; GPS enabled Homelink; Parking sensors; Blind spot warning; Lane departure warning; Power-folding and heated side mirrors; Automatic emergency braking"

> **For buyers of Certified Pre-Owned cars:** A frequent question from prospective owners is "does navigation work if I don't buy the Tech Package?" Yes and no. You **DO** get maps on the touchscreen, the ability to search for locations using voice or keyboard, traffic information, and your car's location superimposed on the moving map. You **DON'T** get turn-by-turn directions, a route overlaid on the map, or navigation in the instrument cluster.

Ultra High Fidelity Sound

(Also known as Premium Sound in early cars.) The Ultra High Fidelity Sound system provides 12 speakers along with electronics that have been engineered to provide the best sound given the interior characteristics of Model S.

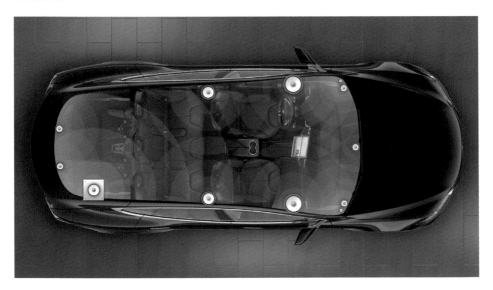

Image © Tesla Motors. Used with permission.

The jury seems to be out on this one. Some people love it; some say there's little difference. Everybody has a different ear for music, and buying this option is very much a matter of personal taste. I didn't choose it, and I don't miss it.

MAYBE

Panoramic Roof

The pano roof provides an "outdoor feel inside the car." The roof over the front seat slides backward over the rear seat area, providing a significant opening for ventilation and viewing from the rear seats. The opening mechanism is

Image © Tesla Motors. Used with permission.

smooth and quiet, providing a quality feel. When closed, the roof blocks 98 percent of visible light and 81 pecent of transmitted heat.

When opened wide, the pano roof increases the level of wind noise substantially, and this is something that some drivers may find irritating.

> Wow your friends by using a very cool graphic on the touchscreen to control the roof. A clearly marked position on the slider will minimize wind noise.

Actually, the roof is far more impressive for those passengers who ride in the rear seat, because the roof's full expanse is easily noticed. When you ride up front, it's not noticable unless you look straight up.

As I mentioned earlier in the book, some buyers worry about heat transmission through the pano roof in hot, high sun climates. Experience indicates this shouldn't be a concern and that the pano roof provides excellent attenuation of the sun's rays while still providing an open-space.

> **More specifically, reports from owners in Florida, Arizona, and California all confirm Tesla's assertion that heat gain through the panoramic roof is not noticable.**

Another consideration for the pano roof is headroom. I'm 6ft. tall and don't have a problem with the solid roof headroom, but some taller owners and those with longer torsos have had problems—especially in the 2nd row of seats. Conversely, I know at least one 6' 4" owner who doesn't have any problems at all.

> The pano roof gives an extra 2–4 inches of headroom and is worth considering for that reason alone. Try and do a test drive if you are the least bit concerned. Also remember that you'll need the pano roof if you want to fit Tesla's roof rack.

I didn't choose the pano roof, and I don't miss it.

MAYBE

Smart Air Suspension

The air suspension provides four main functions:

- The core suspension function, somewhat better than coil springs and dampers.
- Auto-leveling to compensate for heavy loads in the front or rear trunks;
- Auto-lowering the car at highway speeds to improve range (by lowering drag caused by turbulence under the car)
- Manual height adjustment for clearing obstacles (e.g., steep driveway entrances), or easier ingress/egress.

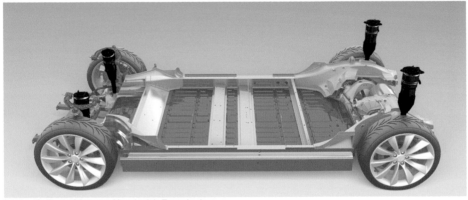

Image © Tesla Motors. Used with Permission.

Everyone with standard suspension likes it; everyone with air prefers it. I've driven both and I think the air suspension is less harsh. If you have a high driveway entry, then air might be helpful.

✓ BUY

Range Upgrade _____

In July 2015 Tesla introduced the 90 kWh battery pack as a $3000 upgrade to the 85 kWh pack. The pack was introduced in preparation for the launch of the Model X SUV. At the time of writing EPA testing had not been completed, but Tesla suggests that the pack will give an extra 6-7% in range.

MAYBE

High Power Wall Connector/Twin Chargers_____

This option differs slightly between North America and Europe.

Image © Tesla Motors. Used with permission.

In North America the HPWC and Twin Chargers come bundled as the *High Power Home Charging* option. Together they provide home charging at 80 A, giving 20 kW of power and 58 miles or range per hour charging. Twin Chargers can also be used with any Level 2 public charger that is capable of delivering up to 20 kW.

At the time of writing, the HPWC has not been released in Europe, and so the Twin Chargers are available on their own.

For many owners, especially those with 85 kWh batteries, this is a nice-to-have feature rather than a must have. Consider the HPWC only if you'll need to charge very quickly when you arrive home with the car empty, or if you'll need 20 kW charging when you are out and about. Note that to get anything above 10 kW charging **you will need twin on-board chargers** (unless you are Supercharging, which bypasses the on-board chargers completely).

MAYBE

Rear Facing (3ʳᵈ row) Child Seats. _____

These are designed for kids up to
about ten years old. Most owners
love them, though some have
reported a variety of problems:
lack of ventilation/overheating;
headlights from following cars
shining in the kids' eyes; lack of
headroom; and problems with
motion sickness.

Despite this, the majority of owners with rear facing child seats seem to think
they are a worthwhile investment.

MAYBE

Other Smaller Options _____

Carbon Fiber Spoiler. Only available on the
P85D. For all intents and purposes, this
feature is purely cosmetic. It provides a
very small amount of down force at high
speeds.

Image © Tesla Motors. Used with permission.

MAYBE

Subzero Weather Package. You'll know if you need it by glancing at an
outdoor thermometer and looking out of the window during winter months. It
includes heated rear seats, wiper blade defrosters and washer nozzle
heaters.

✓ BUY

Premium Front Console. Provides a console that resides in the center channel area between the front seats and provides a place to store small items and additional, more easily accessible, cup holders.

At the time of writing this was only available from the Tesla online store and was not a configurable item when ordering the car. Price includes installation by Tesla service.

Image © Tesla Motors. Used with permission.

The lack of a center console was one of the biggest complaints when the car was first introduced, but after driving the car for a couple of weeks many owners love the extra space. It is a great place to put a handbag, or anything you happen to be carrying. It avoids having things roll around in the foot well.

The Premium Front Console is provided only with black upholstery and a touch of piano black trim. Aftermarket alternatives enable you to configure a center console for your specific upholstery color and trim choice. See Chapter17, Customizing and Accessorizing, Center Console.

There is also a Premium Rear Console.

MAYBE

My Personal Suggestions _____

Here's a more concise summary of what options I think you need, which options are nice to have, and the ones that you can skip.

Exterior Trim	
Paint Color	Very much a personal choice. Multi-coat red is the most popular. I went for Pearl-White. Blue looks almost black in most lights.
Wheels	I love the look of the 21-inch wheels—and grey looks fantastic against Pearl-White. Others really love the 19's. 21's reduce range by approximately 3%.
Panoramic Roof	Those who have it like it; those who don't, don't miss it. Note: it is required for the roof rack.
Interior Trim	
Textile or Leather	Textile is cheaper; I prefer leather.
Regular leather seats vs. next generation seats	Next generation seats are much more supportive.
Leather Color	Again a personal choice. I went with tan.
Alcantara Headliner	Very much a "nice-to-have."
Premium interior package	Another "nice-to-have."
Premium Center Console	Don't order it with the car unless you really, really must have it. Drive for a while with the open console, and only buy the Premium Console if you really need it.

Driving	
Dual Motor	Adds all-wheel drive and improves efficiency. I recommend it.
Smart Air Suspension	I have it. It improves the ride and helps when hauling heavy loads. Useful for steep driveway transitions.
Autopilot	Definitely.
Range Upgrade	Not needed for most drivers.
Charging	
HPWC (and 2nd Charger)	If you need to charge in a *real* hurry without a Supercharger.
Other	
Subzero Weather Package	Notice this isn't a handling package. You'll know if you need it.
Ultra High Fidelity Sound	Some people love it; others can hardly tell the difference. Personally I don't think it's worth it.
Rear Facing Child Seats	Cool for small kids, but they can be hot in the sun and headlights from following cars can be a problem.

Postponing Your Options Choices

Virtually NO options are available as aftermarket selections and can ONLY be chosen at the time of initial order. Make sure you think very carefully about your configuration choices.

Special note about Rear Facing Seats: The 3rd row of seats requires special reinforcement to the rear structure of Model S to increase crash protection. It is therefore *impossible* to add 3rd row seats to cars that are not ordered with them.

6 Considering the Financial Issues

Pricing the car_____

Tesla has taken a somewhat different approach to selling and servicing Model S than almost every other car manufacturer. The key characteristics of Tesla's approach are:

1. **Cutting out the middle man**. Tesla has no dealer network. All stores and service centers are owned by Tesla Motors, and staffed by Tesla employees.

2. **No commission on sales or service.** Store and service employees are salaried. There is no incentive to be a "pushy salesman" or to add extra parts or procedures when servicing a vehicle. Further, service is an "at cost" operation—Tesla deliberately doesn't make profit on their service business.

3. **Warranty coverage is not dependent on regular servicing.** The car's warranty is not dependent on the car being serviced, though it is strongly recommended. The battery warranty even covers owner error.

4. **You pay what you see on the invoice.** Tesla doesn't offer discounts on new cars, or factory rebates.

5. **You order online.** Use the web-based configurator to choose your model, your colors, and your options. Push a button and the car is added to the production schedule.

Pricing the car is therefore very straightforward. You choose your options on the web-based configurator, and the price you see is the price you pay.

Or not quite. Many national and local (state, province or city) governments offer electric vehicle incentives—typically a tax break. In the US there is (at the time of writing) a $7,500 federal tax credit. US states and other countries offer different incentives. The configurator shows these incentives wherever possible.

Leasing or Financing a Model S_____

At their website, Tesla provides the following description of their U.S. leasing program:

> "Tesla leasing is a three-year program with 10,000, 12,000 or 15,000 annual mileage options. A $5,000 down payment, $695 acquisition fee, and the first month's lease payment is due when picking up your Model S. A $395 disposition fee is required when returning your Model S at the end of your lease.

> "Every lease comes with Tesla's Happiness Guarantee. If you don't like your car for any reason within the first three months, you can return it and your remaining lease obligation is waived. While you cannot immediately lease another Model S, you can upgrade to a higher optioned Model S for a fee to cover the new vs. used value difference."

The lease-end buyout cost of the car is approximately 60 percent of the original value of the vehicle, adjusted for options that you might choose.

As examples, let's consider two different Model S vehicles: the S70D with a base price of approximately $75,500 and the P85D with a base price of approximately $105,000. We are assuming there is no trade-in.

Here is a quick approximate breakdown of costs:

Vehicle	S70D	P85D
Base price	$75,000.00	$105,000.00
Delivery	$1200.00	$1200.00
Total	$76,200.00	$106,200.00
Annual miles:	12000	12000
Down payment:	$5,000.00	$5,000.00
Monthly Payment (excluding sales tax)	$838.00	$1,331.00
Approx. Buy-Out Value	$45,000	$63,000

Obviously, additional added options (increasing the price of the Model S) and other considerations will effect your actual final monthly payment. Full details for leases in the U.S and all other countries can be obtained directly from Tesla Motors.

FINANCING (TAKING OUT A LOAN)

If you finance your car in the US you'll still be eligible for State or Federal electric vehicle tax credits. At the time of writing, Tesla in the US was offering a 72 month loan at a 3% APR, with 10% down. In the UK they were offering 4, 5 or 6 year finance with 15% down. In Canada it appeared[52] to be an interest free 6 year loan with $2500 down. Rather than list the details for every country, I'd suggest checking out the Model S configurator on the Tesla Motors web site, or contact Tesla Motors directly.

Determining your cost of ownership

Elon Musk has been very vocal on the subject of the price of Model S compared to other (non-electric) cars. Specifically he highlights the savings in fuel costs over the lifetime of the car. The simplicity of Model S (e.g., no gearbox, no complex internal combustion engine, many fewer moving parts) also has the potential to be much cheaper to maintain.

FUEL COSTS

Fuel cost savings when driving Model S can be substantial. Overall, savings compared to ICE cars are dictated by the local cost of gasoline, the mileage of the ICE vehicle that your Model S replaced, the local cost per kWh of electricity, and the number of miles you drive each month or year.

> The Tesla Motors website has a great calculator that will help you determine your fuel savings.[53]

By way of example, let's assume:

- you drive 15,000 miles per year (the average in the US),
- fuel is $4.00 per (US) gallon,
- your current car gets 22 mpg, and
- electricity is $0.11 per kWh.

Then over five years you'll spend $2,335 on electricity versus $13,636 on gas—a saving of $11,301.

---

[52] No interest rate was shown on the Canadian configurator page on the Tesla web site.
[53] http://www.teslamotors.com/goelectric#savings

Savings will be greater if gas prices rise faster than electricity costs (likely), or if any of your charging is done at Superchargers or at a location where you don't have to pay (e.g., at work).

MAINTENANCE COSTS

Maintenance costs can add up. Tesla is one of the few car companies that have stated that regular maintenance is NOT a requirement to keep the warranty in force on your car. Maintenance is, however, sensible.

There are two key aspects of maintenance cost that are worth highlighting:

> 1. Tesla services cars using an "at-cost" model. It makes no profit on its maintenance work.

For many car companies, profit from replacement parts used during service can be significant and may in fact outweigh the profit from producing the cars themselves. This is a powerful incentive to recommend parts and service that are not strictly necessary. Tesla's at-cost model eliminates this incentive and will reduce service costs on a like-for-like basis.

> 2. The powertrain of Model S is significantly simpler and has many fewer moving parts compared to an ICE car, or a hybrid.

An old technology ICE vehicle is a complex machine. Hundreds and hundreds of parts must all work in tandem and the possibility of failures is—well, we've all owned ICE vehicles. Hybrids are arguably even more complex because of the addition of a control system that must coordinate the interplay of fossil and electric power. With a Model S there is less to go wrong, and consequently less to fix.

7 Placing Your Order

You've decided to become a Model S owner. Congratulations! Order-to-delivery is a straightforward six-step process:

1. Choose your options and push the order button
2. Pay your deposit[54]
3. Wait while your car is built to order
4. Agree on a delivery date and location
5. Pay the balance due
6. Take delivery

At some point in the process Tesla should assign you a Delivery Specialist who will guide you through the final stages of the process. Get to know them! They can be a big help if things don't go perfectly.

Here are a few typical questions (and answers) that potential Model S owners have about this process:

Q. How do I choose my options?

If at all possible check out the car at a Tesla store[55] and get a feel for the colors and different trim options. Test-drive the car – ideally a couple of different variants such as 70D and P85D so you can get a feel for the difference. Then go online and place your order. Make sure you've carefully read my options recommendations in Chapter 5.

Q. Can I cancel my order?

The answer may vary in the future, but generally there is a two-week period after you place your order when you can cancel and still get a full refund of your deposit.

Q. Can I change options after I've placed my order?

It depends. If you contact Tesla Motors customer service before your status page shows "the factory is sourcing parts" you may be okay, though at the time of writing Tesla seemed to be implementing a policy change whereby

---

[54] Then go back change your options every hour until the two-week deadline is up!
[55] You can find the nearest Tesla store to you by visiting: http://www.teslamotors.com/findus

changes had to be locked in within 2 weeks of placing the order. When it shows "sourcing parts" you still might be okay. If you contact Ownership when the page shows "the factory is building your car," you are most likely to have a problem. If you ask really, really nicely, and are really, really insistent then the factory has been known to make exceptions.

Q. How long does it take to get my car?

It depends on what you order and where you are. Dates are changing all the time so it is impossible to give a definitive answer, but remember that all cars are built to order (unless you purchase a loaner vehicle). In the US, P85D cars are usually delivered within 4-6 weeks of order; other models around 6-12 weeks. In other countries where deliveries have already started, figure on 3-6 months.

Certified Pre-Owned (CPO) cars are available immediately.

Q. Will I lose my deposit?

If you cancel your order after the car has started production, you can probably kiss your deposit goodbye, but there's always a chance that Tesla may be lenient.

Q. Can I buy a Model S for less than full price?

New cars? No. The price you see is the price you pay.

In 2015 Tesla introduced the Certified Pre-Owned (CPO) program to offer used cars with full factory warranty. Used cars are also for sale on places like eBay Motors, and occasionally a luxury car dealer might take one in part exchange. Tesla Motors also sells loaner/demo vehicles—generally reduced in price by $1 for each mile they have driven, and by $1000 for each month of age.

Q. Can I take delivery at the factory?

Yes! And make sure you book a factory tour—it is well worth it!

Q. Can I avoid the delivery charge if I take delivery at the factory?

No.

Q. Can I trade in my car for a new Model S?

This varies by country, but Tesla seems to be putting arrangements in place to do this in every market.

Q. Can I trade in my old Model S for a new Model S?

Almost certainly, but be prepared to be offered no more than the original price less $1 per mile and $1000 per month of age.

Q. Is Model S expensive to insure?

Not necessarily. It is a relatively expensive vehicle so it is likely that your insurance costs will not be rock bottom, but if you search around it is possible to insure Model S for no more than—and in some cases quite a bit less than—equivalent (performance) sedans.

8 Planning Your Personal Charging Infrastructure

Charging is an activity that you'll do almost every day. In essence, you'll treat your Model S much like you treat your smart phone: plug it in at night and have a full[56] battery every morning. The cool thing about this is that your car is full every time you leave your garage or driveway—no more gas stations!

Model S comes with a charging cable—the Universal Mobile Connector, or "UMC"—that plugs into the car and your electrical outlet. While it is possible to charge Model S from a "regular" 110V or Schuko electrical outlet, the vast majority of owners install a dedicated outlet, which can often be done for a few hundred dollars.

You'll need to decide where you want to plug in, the type of circuit your desire, who is going to do the work, and when they're going to do it. By the way, all of this should be done *before* you take delivery of the vehicle.

Charging solutions vary from country to country, and I'll cover the major options here. Make sure you check out the section on "Customizing Your Garage" on page 163 for a few real-world examples of owners' charging setups.

It helps (but it isn't necessary) to have a basic understanding of voltage (measured in Volts) and current (measured in Amps) and how each of these relates to power (measured in Watts) and energy (measured in Watt-hours). For an explanation of these terms see "Volts, Amps and all that electrical jargon" in Chapter 20.

North America

In North America, you have a number of home charging options:

110V/12A or 220V/10A outlets. This is a "typical" outlet you'll find in a home or garage. If at all possible avoid using 110V! Charging is very, very, slow, (it will take more than 2 days to charge your car from empty) and very, very inefficient. Based on info from the charging section of the Tesla website page, you'll use 132 kWh to fill an 85 kWh battery.

---

[56] Tesla strongly recommends that you do not charge to 100% regularly. You can set a daily charging limit, which is typically 80-90%.

220V, 50A, NEMA 14-50 Circuit. Most Model S owners use a 220V, 50A NEMA 14-50 outlet. This charges the car at 40A,[57] and gives about 28 miles for every hour it is plugged in. This is generally sufficient for most users and is an inexpensive circuit to install in your garage. The only real problem you might encounter is if you own an older house with limited electric service (i.e., 100A service), or if you live in an apartment building with a shared garage. In the former case you may need an electric service upgrade—an expensive remodeling activity that requires a competent electrician.

> The installation of a 50A NEMA 14-50 circuit should be done by a competent electrician. Cost will vary depending on the physical location, the number of feet of electric cable that need to be run, and any routing complexity that an electrician might encounter. In general, costs will range between $500 for simple installation to well over $1500 for complex, longer installations.

If you're a competent electrical do-it-yourselfer *and* you're comfortable installing electric circuits coming from your service breaker box, it is possible to install a NEMA 14-50 circuit yourself.[58] The materials you'll need are relatively simple: #6 electrical cable, a NEMA 14-50 receptacle and box, conduit for your garage wall, and a 50A circuit breaker. Depending on the length of cable you'll need, this job should cost between $150 and $300 for materials.

High Power Wall Connector (HPWC). The HPWC is a 220V, 80A (20kW) circuit that provides you with the fastest home charging for your Model S. Some owners also like the permanent installation of the HPWC.

---

[57] In the US, electrical code requires that "continuous load" circuits, such as those used for BEV charging, are limited to 80% of rated load. So a 50A circuit can only be used at 40A.

[58] A DIY charging circuit installation should be attempted ONLY if you are a competent electrical installer with sufficient experience in circuit installations. You must follow all local codes and be absolutely comfortable with 230V–240V installations emanating from your service box. If you have any doubts whatsoever, hire a competent electrician!

> **IMPORTANT: You *can* use the HPWC if you have a single charger in your Model S, but you *must* have twin chargers to get more than 10kW from the HPWC.**

If you need rapid charging on a regular basis (e.g., you arrive home with a low battery at 3:00pm and need to prepare your Model S for a long trip leaving at 6:00pm), the HPWC is a good option. You'll need to install a 100-amp circuit and have the electrical service to support it.

In my opinion, the HPWC is overkill for most Model S owners, though it does look good on the wall.

Mainland Europe/Scandinavia

In Europe, your home charging options are:

- 5-pin IEC 60309 adapter (red)—provides three phase 400 VAC charging at 16A and delivers 55 kilometers of range per hour.

- 3-pin IEC 60309 adapter (blue)—provides single-phase 230 VAC charging at 10-32A and delivers up to 40 kilometers of range per hour.

- Standard "Schuko" adapter provides 230V at 13A (14 km/h)

- 7-pin IEC 62196 Type-2 adapter (blue)—provides single phase 230 VAC at 16 or 32A delivering 18 or 36 km of range per hour, or three phase 400 VAC at 16 or 32A delivering 55 or 110 km of range per hour.

- At the time of writing the HPWC is not available in Europe, but may become available during 2015.

Note that the 400 V/32A option requires dual chargers in the car to achieve anything more than 55 km of range per hour.

United Kingdom

In the UK, your home charging options are:

- 7-pin IEC 62196 Type-2 adapter (blue)—provides single phase 230 VAC at 16 or 32A delivering 11 or 22 miles of range per hour, or three phase 400 VAC at 16 or 32A delivering 34 or 68 miles of range per hour.

- At the time of writing the HPWC is not available in the UK, but may become available during 2015.

Note that the 400 V/32A option requires dual chargers in the car to achieve anything more than 34 miles of range per hour.

Other countries

Please check the Tesla Motors website for charging information and specifications for other countries.

Summary of Tesla Charging Options

The image below summarizes the different charging options available from Tesla in Europe and North America. Charging rates vary by more than a factor of 100, so it helps to understand what's available. Check out Chapter 19 on Superchargers to learn more about how Tesla achieves the very high charging rates, and the tips to minimize your charging time.

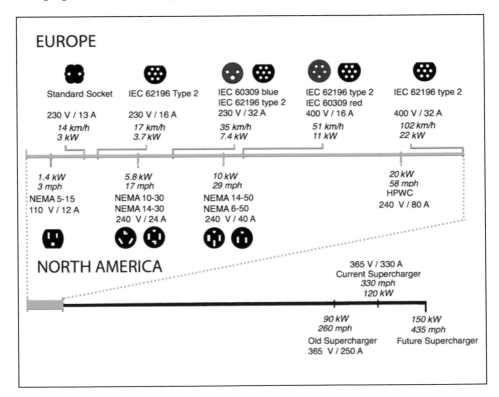

Installing the Charging Circuit_____

WARNING: A DIY charging circuit installation should be attempted ONLY if you are a competent electrical installer with sufficient experience in circuit installations. You must follow all local codes and be absolutely comfortable with 230V–240V installations emanating from your service box. If you have any doubts whatsoever, hire a competent electrician!

IF YOU USE AN ELECTRICIAN

Tesla supplies installation instructions for both the NEMA 14-50 outlet and the HPWC. You can find them both on the Manuals pages on the Tesla website. [59,60]

IF YOU DECIDE TO DO THE INSTALL YOURSELF

Make sure the electrical feed into your house has enough capacity, and that there is room for a new circuit in your panel! If you don't know what the last sentence means—Stop! You shouldn't be doing the install.

Later in the book, we'll discuss the potential of electrical fires and overheating from badly installed charging solutions. Though rare, the danger is real and the consequences can be serious.

Forum user @FlasherZ created an all-you-need-to-know thread[61] at Tesla Motors Club (TMC) detailing installation instructions. Some of the key points are:

- There are three important factors: **Will it work? Is it safe? Is it legal?** Make sure you understand the differences and act accordingly.

- **Do I need a building permit?** Probably. Check with your local city/ county/ parish.

- **Can I use an old dryer outlet?**[62] Check the adapter guide on the Tesla website to help identify what you have. Most likely you'll need to limit your

---

[59] http://www.teslamotors.com/sites/default/files/downloads/universalmobileconnector_ nema_14-50.pdf
[60] http://www.teslamotors.com/sites/default/files/downloads/highpowerwallconnector.pdf
[61] http://www.teslamotorsclub.com/showthread.php/12615-FAQ-Home-Tesla-charging-infrastructure-Q-amp-A
[62] In North America, clothes dryers typically use a 220V, 30A outlet than the usual 110V.

PLANNING YOUR PERSONAL CHARGING INFRASTRUCTURE

charging current, and because of wiring differences you may run into problems.

- **Can I create my own adapter?** Yes, but be very, very careful. There are comprehensive (unofficial) instructions available.[63] Where possible use official Tesla UMC adapters.

- **Can I combine two 120V outlets into one 240V circuit?** In theory, but there are several caveats. Read the instructions on the TMC site.

- **Can I use an extension cord?** Tesla says no. In practice it is possible to use an extension cord if it is rated appropriately, but again there are caveats.

- **Should I contact my power company?** Yes—to make sure there are no issues with the load you are adding (especially it if is the HPWC), and to find out if there are any discounts or incentives available.

- **At what height should I install the outlet?** Anything between 18 inches and 4 feet from the floor. Think about how you will route the cable to your car. (Along the floor? Up and over?) Make sure that you take the mounting location for your outlet into account when planning. Think about where you're going to park the car—front in vs. reversing in, and so forth.

> Note that the included charging cable (known as the UMC or Universal Mobile Connector) is 20 feet long, with the first 2 feet taken up with a "pigtail" and the controller, so there are about 18 feet of usable cable.

By the way, it's okay to leave the UMC plugged into the wall when not in use. It draws virtually zero current and avoids wear and tear from constantly unplugging/ plugging.

INSTALLATION WHEN YOUR RESIDENCE ISN'T A SINGLE-FAMILY HOME

If you have a condominium or live in an apartment building, installation of an appropriate circuit for charging may be considerably more difficult and appreciably more expensive. One Model S owner in my area had to run almost 400 feet of underground cable from his condo to his parking spot. The cost was over $8,000! He had to battle his condo board and local building inspector, but he got the job done. Although that's an extreme case,

---

[63] http://cosmacelf.net/Home%20Made%20Adapters.pdf

expect additional installation challenges if you don't live in a single-family house.

There is some good news though. Some states (such as California) and some countries have enacted laws to encourage or mandate condo associations and/or freeholders to agree to the installation of electric vehicle charging stations.

If you keep your car in a commercial parking garage or use on-street parking, you'll also face challenges. Getting the garage owner to install an appropriate circuit may be difficult and quite expensive. If you regularly park on the street, your best charging option may be at your place of work, using publically available charging facilities, or a Tesla Supercharger.

9 Delivery Day—Checklists

Model S owners will tell you that they reacted to delivery day in the same way that an 8-year old reacts to Christmas morning. There's excitment, anticipation, impatience and yes, even a little fear about your decision. It's a day you won't soon forget.

Here's how to handle it.

Your delivery date can change—be ready! _____

DO NOT get fixated on a specific delivery day/time. Your Model S *may come early* or be delayed. The two biggest delay reasons are, "the car is on a truck and the truck is stuck in XYZ; it will be another week..." or delays due to inspections or rework on the manufacturing line. On the positive side you may get, "I know we said it would be delivered next week, but it's already here. Can we deliver it tomorrow?"

My advice: get everything (including financing and charging) ready early just in case you get a nice surprise and have an early delivery.

Preparing for delivery_____

You've got charging ready to go, right? No? Go back and read Chapter 8. Note that you'll need time to schedule an electrician if you have to install a new circuit or outlet.

The only things you might want to have handy when you take delivery are:

- Your phone (to test in the car and take lots of pictures/videos)
- A friend to take photos/videos for you
- A USB stick with some music
- This book—but don't plan on reading it during the delivery. You'll be too busy!

In case your Tesla Delivery Specialist can't make it, or you live in a state where this is problematic, the official Tesla Motors video walkthrough can be found at: http://www.teslamotors.com/support

What you'll need _____

There's remarkably little that you need during delivery—the main thing being the payment (assuming you are not in a state or country that requires payment *before* delivery). Tesla will take a personal check, but make sure you've got the funds in the bank—it will probably clear within 24 hours.

What to look for when the car comes off the trailer _____

Based on customer reports, Model S is delivered with remarkably few quality problems and issues, but production and delivery problems can crop up occasionally

If you can contain your excitement about taking delivery of your Model S, you should start by checking for basic problems that others have encountered:

*   *Dirt under the clear coat*
*   *Scratches in the paint*
*   *Windshield distortion or cracks* (especially near the passenger side A-pillar half way up). Distortion in the lower 1 inch is normal, cracks are not!
*   *Underside damage from loading/unloading*
*   *Wheel scrapes*
*   *Tire scrapes* (my sidewall was damaged)
*   *Black, sticky "goop" on the windows or on the sunroof.* The felt seal may have come free and the glue/sealant is sticking to the window.
*   *Misaligned hood or trunk lid.* Service can usually adjust this without issues.
*   *Dirt/smudges on headliner/seats/trim from delivery driver*

If you see significant problems—such as those with the paintwork—it is up to you whether you stop the delivery at that point, or carry on.

Once you give the car a quick once over, it's time to get considerably more detailed. The following pages (among the most important in this book) present a detailed checklist that will help you to make delivery a success.

Basic checklist

- ☐ Is it your car? (Believe it or not, someone had the wrong car delivered)
- ☐ Make sure the VIN matches the paperwork
- ☐ Correct battery size? (Press the Tesla "T" on the 17" screen to see details. There's also a sticker at the back of the passenger side front wheel well.)
- ☐ Correct paint color?
- ☐ Correct leather/interior color/trim?
- ☐ Correct wheels?
- ☐ Correct tires? (Especially if Michelin Primacies were ordered.)
- ☐ Correct roof? (Solid color or panoramic)
- ☐ Two keys
- ☐ Temporary tags
- ☐ Tire inflation kit (if mandatory in your state/country)
- ☐ Front and rear floor mats
- ☐ Chrome "Tesla" license plate frame (check the frunk if you can't find it)
- ☐ Front license plate mount (check the frunk if you can't find it; see the "other things to do" section below for alternate mounting solutions)
- ☐ Printed manuals (in glove box)
- ☐ Universal Mobile Connector (UMC) cable with standard adapters and carry bag
- ☐ North America:
  - ☐ J1772 adapter
  - ☐ NEMA 5-15 110V adapter
  - ☐ NEMA 14-50 240V adapter
  - ☐ NEMA 6-50 adapter (only if the High Power Wall Connector has been ordered and not yet delivered)
- ☐ Europe:
  - ☐ Schuko adapter
  - ☐ IEC 60309 Red or Blue depending on choice, or IEC 62196
- ☐ Cover for the well in trunk (see problems, below)
- ☐ Latest software version (Press the Tesla "T" on the 17" screen to see details. Check the www.teslamotorsclub.com website)
- ☐ P85D, 85D, 85, 70 or 70D badge on the rear of the car (occasionally some are delivered without badges)

Optional Items _____

Check installed options against purchased options on your paperwork:

- ❏ Wheels
    - ❏ 19" Standard
    - ❏ 19" Cyclone
    - ❏ 19" Dark Grey Cyclone (only available in specific countries)
    - ❏ 21" Silver Turbine
    - ❏ 21" Dark Grey Turbine
- ❏ Tesla Red Brake Calipers
- ❏ Tech package (Check this by seeing if you have Navigation, auto-dimming mirrors)
- ❏ Ultra High Fidelity Sound package
- ❏ Leather Seats
- ❏ Enhanced Seats (Check for larger bolsters)
- ❏ Extended Napa Leather Trim
- ❏ Alcantara Headliner
- ❏ Premium Interior Lighting
- ❏ Air suspension (Check the option on the main controls screen)
- ❏ Supercharging option
- ❏ Rear facing child seats
- ❏ Parcel Shelf
- ❏ Fog Lamps
- ❏ Carbon Fiber Spoiler
- ❏ Sub Zero Weather Package
- ❏ Yacht Floor
- ❏ Premium Center Console
- ❏ Paint Armor
- ❏ Security Package (Europe Only)
- ❏ Second set of wheels (usually for winter tires)
- ❏ High Performance Wall Charger and Twin (in-car) Chargers

Now make sure everything works correctly _____

☐ All doors close properly (a few users have reported door misalignment).

☐ All handles work properly (various handle problems reported).

> *In rare cases, this is a mechanical problem that requires replacing the handle, though some users have reported that problems can sometimes be resolved by taking out the appropriate fuse (number 32, 40 or 41—check the Model S Owner's Manual) for five minutes then replacing it.*

☐ Windows auto-close the last inch when closing the door.

> *If there's a problem, try lowering the window all the way down, and then all the way up; this may reset the sensor.*

☐ Charge Port Cover opens and closes consistently.

> *Open and close the cover using both the physical button on the UMC and the virtual button in the car display. (Cars built before October 2014 had manual-closing port covers)*

☐ UMC latches and unlatches without problems, and charging works.

> *Even if you are taking delivery at the Service Center, make sure you try your own UMC cable. Bad chargers / cables have been reported. Make sure you try 110V, 240V and all adapters. Ensure the green light comes on the UMC when you plug it into the wall. It is better to make sure it works before you get home.*

> *Make sure you push the cable in. It takes a bit of getting used to and can require more force than you might first assume. It can feel like it is in when it has stopped part way. You'll know when it is in properly when the ring or lights turn green.*

☐ Windshield jets do not point too low.

> *Can be adjusted using a pin in the jet. Be sure that windshield washer fluid tank has been filled.*

❑ Tire Pressures are okay.

High pressures (54 psi) have been reported at delivery. Check the label on the driver-side B-pillar to get the right pressure for your car. Pressures differ for 19" and 21" wheels, air and coil suspension, and the Performance model.

❑ Radio reception is okay.

❑ Smart Phone contacts syncing and Bluetooth music streaming.

Owners have been able to get most phones to work, even clamshell phones. If you are unable to pair, it could be a Bluetooth problem. Let Tesla Service and your Delivery Specialist know.

❑ Rear seat belts slide freely.

The left and right rear seat belts can sometimes scrape/drag when you pull them. This is a faulty/missing part problem and there is a known fix for it. Tesla has to order a new part.

When you get home:

❑ Set up HomeLink for garage door(s).

Some people have found this to be difficult. If you are having problems, hold your remote inside the middle of the frunk (front trunk) when you are trying to program the car. Alternatively try against the front lip of the frunk and on the frunk floor, 2 inches to the driver's side of the frunk light.

Other problems that have been reported _____

☐ Condensation in the rear lights/reflectors.

> *Been reported by quite a few people. Annoying, but doesn't seem to cause any problems, per se. Tesla has new seals that will fix this problem.*

☐ Low frequency powerful rumbling when first turned on.

> *This is the A/C compressor vibrating against the frunk liner. Service has a fix whereby they reposition the mounting bracket.*

☐ 12V battery failures.

> *Model S uses a 12V battery to power the instruments, lights, etc.*
>
> *More importantly it is used to power the mechanical "contactors" that connect the main battery to the drive train (that is the "clunk" you hear when you turn on). Therefore, if the 12V battery fails or is flat, YOU CANNOT START THE CAR. Also, the parking brake will be locked on. You will need to attach a 12V supply to the posts behind the nose to avoid having to drag the car with the wheels locked.*

If you receive any 12V warnings, or your car is non-responsive IMMEDIATELY CALL TESLA SERVICE. They or the ranger can replace the battery.

☐ Inoperable map lights. A few users have reported problems with the map lights. You might not realize it but each one can be pressed to turn on/off. A handful of users reported problems at delivery or after a few days. Give them all a push and make sure they work!

☐ A very small number of owners have reported issues that have been caused by loose fuses. If you or your Delivery Specialist feel so inclined, it might be worth popping off the fuse cover in the frunk (the *Model S Owner's Manual* shows how to do it) and making sure all the fuses are seated properly.

What do you want to set-up first? _____

The first thing you'll want to do (with the help of your Delivery Specialist, if possible) is to set up basic components:

- Driver profile
- HomeLink
- Instrument Cluster Displays
- Creep Mode
- Regen Mode
- Traction Control

- Phone Syncing
- Audio Favorites
- Right Scroll Wheel
- Steering Mode
- Sport/Insane/Ludicrous Mode
- Wi-Fi connection at home

These are some of the more common items that you should focus on, but there are many other settings that control navigation, lighting, driver assist, suspension and other aspects of the vehicle that you can adjust. To help you prepare for the set-up, I've included information below on the most common settings and where you'll find them on the display, along with a few tips and comments. These instructions are correct up through software version 6.x, but may change with subsequent versions.

DRIVER PROFILE

Driver profiles save A LOT more than just seat and mirror positions; there's a link on the driver profiles page that shows what gets saved/restored. Set up a profile for yourself and anyone else who drives the car.

If you and your significant other have large height differences it can be difficult to get into the car if the other person has the seat a long way forward. There is a simple solution.

> **Set up an "Exit" profile that positions the seat all the way back. When the "short" driver exits the car, he/she can hit "Exit" so the next driver can enter the car comfortably.**

PHONE SYNCING

Phone syncing and pairing are pretty straightforward. Owners have been able to pair most types of phones. Model S occasionally forgets contact information; the simplest fix is to press the Bluetooth icon and push the "connect" button. Occasionally it may be necessary to reboot the main computer. See "Rebooting the displays—why and how?" on page 125. The icon turns blue when a device is connected.

HOMELINK

HomeLink (remote control of garage doors) is accessed from the top  navigation bar of the touchscreen. HomeLink in Model S is GPS aware—it will remember where it was programmed and will automatically present the menu when you arrive at that location.

Because of this, you should program HomeLink wherever you'd like the menu to trigger. For example, if you have a gate opener to your neighborhood, don't program the car at work!

> If you are having problems programming HomeLink, hold your garage remote inside the middle of the frunk when you are trying to program the car. Alternatively place the remote against the front lip of the frunk, or on the frunk floor 2 inches to the driver's side of the frunk light.

AUDIO FAVORITES

Up through software version 6.1, the Audio interface is possibly the weakest part of the Model S user interface. I find it overly complex and confusing, partly due to the range of audio sources: AM, FM (and in Europe, DAB) radio, TuneIn radio, Slacker radio, and Sirius Satellite (with the Ultra High Fidelity audio package).

In each source it is possible to save multiple favorite stations. These appear on a single favorites menu that can become very long and unwieldy. I've yet to uncover any "best practice" approaches to this, and there are no tweaks you can make to control the order of favorites or any renaming of favorites.

One tweak you *can* do is to use your own premium Slacker credentials. This allows you to access in the car playlists you create elsewhere. Until Tesla improves the user interface, you just have to do the best you can.

INSTRUMENT CLUSTER DISPLAYS

The instrument cluster has two configurable areas, to the left and right of the speedometer. The left area will show a moving map when navigating[64] but can be configured to show other displays when not. The right area is configurable at all times.

My preference is to show the energy meter in the left area, and the media info in the right area.

Press and hold each scroll wheel to choose which display you want to use.

---

[64] Requires the Tech Package on pre-2015 cars

RIGHT SCROLL WHEEL

The left scroll wheel always controls the media/phone volume, but the right wheel can be programmed to control one of several items including:

1. Screen brightness
2. Panoramic roof percent
3. Fan speed
4. Media source
5. Climate Temperature

Press the button below the scroll wheel to bring up the configuration menu.

CREEP MODE: ON OR OFF?

"Creep" recreates the behavior of an automatic transmission ICE car—the car will "creep" forwards or backwards without pressing the accelerator pedal. I spent the first six months with Creep turned on. Since then I've turned it off—I find it is easier to do "one foot driving" because I don't need to hold the car on the brake at every stop.

STEERING: STANDARD, SPORT OR COMFORT?

I started on Sport, but ultimately switched to Comfort—it makes the car feel lighter. A poll on the TM Forum suggested that the majority of owners prefer standard mode.

REGEN: STANDARD OR LOW

Most owners find Standard regen to work best. It enables "one foot driving"—using regen to slow the car rather than using the brake. You'll get used to it very quickly, and you'll wonder why all cars don't work  that way. However, there are situations such as freeway driving in which low regen results in a more comfortable driving experience. If I'm doing a long freeway trip I'll often toggle to "Low" once I'm on the freeway.

ACCELERATION: SPORT OR INSANE/LUDICROUS

The P85D has an option button to choose between "Sport" acceleration or "Insane" acceleration (or "Ludicrous" if you have that option). Tesla has not  specified the exact difference between these two settings, but the acceleration in Sport mode seems to give a 0-60 time closer to 4.1 seconds versus the 3.1 seconds in Insane mode or the 2.8 in Ludicrous mode.

TRACTION CONTROL: ON OR OFF?

This one is a no-brainer. Model S, even in the base S70 configuration, has huge amounts of torque and it will easily spin the wheels—or the car if you aren't  careful. The system shows a warning when you try to turn traction control off, for good reason. (P85D cars have a "slip start" option rather than an on/off option.)

WINDSHIELD WIPERS: AUTO OR NOT?

This is very much a personal choice. I have mine set to the first auto setting.

A word of warning, however. The rain sensing mechanism is quite sensitive and as a consequence, will sometimes wipe when a leaf or other small object hits the windshield. Normally this isn't a problem, but a friend once parked under a tree that dropped a very fine mist of sticky sap on the windshield. After it dried, a leaf fell on the windshield after he started his Model S. The wipers started up, got stuck on the sap and stripped the wiper gearing. An unusual event to be sure, but worth noting.

CONNECT TO HOME WI-FI

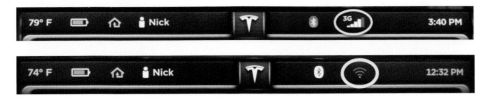

Starting with software version 5.6, Tesla turned on Wi-Fi connectivity. Assuming you have sufficient signal strength your car should be able to connect to your home Wi-Fi network. Where your Wi-Fi signal is stronger than the car's 3G signal this may facilitate downloading of software updates. Press the "3G" (or "LTE") icon on the status bar to bring up the Wi-Fi settings. When Wi-Fi is enabled the "3G" icon will change to a signal strength icon.

What questions to ask?

The following questions are well worth asking when the Delivery Specialist is present. Sure, you can dig the information out of the *Model S Owner's Manual* (in most cases) but a personal demo is far easier, and often considerably more illuminating.

1. **How does charging work? What do the colors on the charge port mean?**
   a. Pulsing White—ready
   b. Pulsing Yellow—UMC not fully inserted
   c. Solid Blue—connected and communicating
   d. Pulsing Green—charging (can take a minute or two to start)
   e. Solid Green—charged up
   f. Red—Failure (possibly hardware)

2. **How do I operate the windshield wipers?** This can take some practice. The wipers are located behind the steering wheel spoke, and as a consequence, are not directly visible for some drivers. The rotation direction of the wiper control is unusual, so setting them to the right operation may be confusing at first.

3. **How do I connect Model S to a Wi-Fi network (v5.x or above software required) and ensure that signal strength is adequate for updates?** This is very straightforward, but Wi-Fi signal strength in your garage or driveway can be a problem.

4. **Can you provide a demo of all functionality in steering wheel thumb switches?**
   a. Phone controls
   b. Audio/music controls
   c. How to change what the steering wheel switches control
   d. Other
5. **How do I modify the displays that appear next to the speedometer?**
   a. What options do I have?
   b. What displays are most important for most drivers?
6. **What are the Traffic Aware Cruise Control settings?**
7. **How do I adjust seat, mirrors, save driver profile(s)?** Most of this is relatively straightforward, but setting the side mirror auto-adjustment for backing up is not.

> To set the mirrors for reverse, (1) put the car in reverse, (2) use the Driver Profile button at the top of the display to select the driver, (3) set the mirrors, and (4) save.

8. **Can you provide a demo of the cruise control functionality?**
9. **How is vehicle status information displayed (e.g., tire pressure warning)?**
10. **Can you please walk through all screen displays and explain what I'm seeing?**
11. **Can you help me download the iPhone/Android app and then demo its use?**

   The Tesla iPhone App available is in the Apple App Store.[65]

   The Tesla Android app is available in the Google Play Store[66]

   There is no official Tesla app on Windows Phone.

---

[65] https://itunes.apple.com/us/app/tesla-model-s/id582007913?mt=8
[66] https://play.google.com/store/apps/details?id=com.teslamotors.tesla&hl=en

What if I find something wrong during delivery?_____

Tell the Delivery Specialist. Depending on the nature of the problem, either get it noted on the due bill, or *in extremis* refuse to accept the car.

> Don't leave (or let the Delivery Specialist leave) until you've been over the car with a fine-tooth comb and you are completely satisfied. Make sure you take a copy of the due bill if you can. These guys are generally very good, so even if there are issues, a good Delivery Specialist will make sure everything gets fixed ASAP.

If you spot anything after you leave, make contact as soon as possible, and make sure you email Ownership so there is a written record. Follow up with a phone call. This is a pretty expensive piece of equipment, and you want it to be perfect.

10 Driving Model S

As I said in the preface, Model S is like every car you've ever owned, and like no car you've ever owned. It is arguably the most spacious, safest, most economical, and highly performing premium sedan on the market.

When it comes to driving, Model S is the ultimate wolf in sheep's clothing. Gentle application of the accelerator gives one of the most relaxing drives out there. Mashing the go pedal unleashes a torrent of power unlike any sedan in the world.

In this chapter I'll discuss how to get the most out of the car, and especially how to get the most out of the battery.

Managing Range

With the introduction of Software Version 6.2 in March 2015, Tesla aims to put an end to range anxiety. New features automatically alert the owner to situations where range may be an issue, and give optimized driving directions via Tesla and public chargers. As Elon tweeted at the time, the goal of 6.2 is to put an end to range anxiety. For this second edition of *Owning Model S* I've decided to retain this section on managing range, though hopefully with 6.2 and subsequent software updates it will become less and less important.

Although we've already discussed range twice in this book, my best advice to you is to *try to stop worrying about it!* Unless you need to go a really long way, or are negligent in your charging habits, or it is freakishly cold, you can pretty much ignore the range meter.

But given that it is (a) the first thing most non-Tesla owners ask about, (b) the most confusing thing about Model S, and (c) the most variable thing about Model S, it is worth going into a bit more detail.

Given the relatively large capacities of the Model S batteries (compared to other battery electric vehicles), range ought not to be a problem. Plus the instrument cluster always shows the available range, so where's the issue?

Rated Range

Many owners set the instrument cluster to display rated range, and this is the default setting. Unfortunately, rated range is NOT how far you can travel. At best it is a close approximation to the state of charge of the battery. At worst, it is misleading and confusing.

The official[67] word from Tesla is that:

> **Rated range is the distance the car will go if your driving style matches the EPA 5-cycle test (North America) or the ECE R101 test (Europe).**

You will only be able to judge your driving style after driving for some time.

Rated Range is different in different markets. In North America, it is based on the EPA "5-cycle test"; in Europe it is based on ECE R101 (also known as NEDC or New European Driving Cycle). These different standards give markedly different results for rated range.

The original "2-cycle" EPA test yielded the magical 300 mile range that Tesla designed the car to achieve (what Tesla now calls "Ideal" or "Typical" range). In May of 2012 the EPA released their 5-cycle test results for Model S that gave a 265-mile range (for the S85 and P85). Tesla adjusted the rated range calculation in North American cars to match this value at 100% ("range") charge.

In Europe, the ECE R101 test yields a 100% charge range of 311 miles, 17% higher than the EPA test. Rated Range in Europe is therefore 311 miles.

> **The Rated Range in North America is 265 miles. In Europe it is 311 miles. This does NOT mean the car will travel any further in absolute terms; it just means the assumptions on which the range is calculated are different.**

So how far can the car travel on a full charge? It depends on your average energy consumption. The energy meter in the car displays energy use in Watt-hours per mile ("Wh/m"). The lower the number, the further you can drive. So what does the number have to be in order to drive 265 miles? After

---

[67] See the "Calculation of Rated Range" thread in the Tesla Motors forum

much experimentation by various owners in North America, the best calculation seems to be that for an 85 kWh car it is 286 Wh/m. In other words:

> **In North America, if your average Wh/m displayed on the energy meter is 286, you'll be able to drive the Rated Range of 265 miles.**

Let's explore the energy graph in the touchscreen:

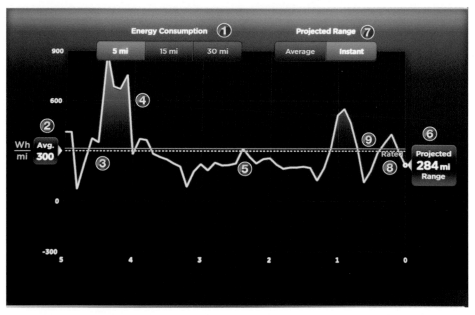

Energy Graph in the touchscreen.

The graph shows your average historical energy use in Wh/m over the last 5, 15 or 30 miles (①) in numeric form (②) and as a dashed horizontal line (③). Peaks (④) correspond to hard acceleration or climbing hills while more level stretches (⑤) correspond to more gentle, lower speed driving. The graph also shows an estimate of your projected range (⑥) based on either (⑦) the 5/15/30 mile average use or your "instant" use (last 1/10ᵗʰ of a mile). The projection will vary as the average changes with your driving style.

Note that this projection is NOT related to rated miles. Rated consumption (⑧) is shown as the solid horizontal line (⑨) *and does not change*. In the graph (taken from my car in the US), the solid rated line (⑨) at 306 Wh/m is slightly above the dashed average line (③) that is currently at 300 Wh/m.

Why then is the "rated range" solid line on the energy meter at 306 Wh/m and not at 286? It's complicated, and I've included an explanation in the section entitled "Battery Pack capacity—what's really available?" in Chapter 20.

> **Bottom line: The range shown in the speedometer is *not necessarily* how far you can drive. Be careful until you get used to the car's behavior.**

For a more detailed explanation of Tesla's range nomenclature, see the section titled "Rated vs. Ideal vs. Typical vs. Projected Range" beginning on page 181.

COLD WEATHER

Nothing seems to affect range quite so much as cold weather. As you drive the car you'll become familiar with how it reacts in a variety of situations, but to avoid being caught without a charge in cold weather follow these "COLD" weather rules:

C **harge Up**—Don't try and cut it too fine. Plan for at least a 25% range buffer—if you need to go 100 miles then charge to at least 125 rated miles. If it is below freezing and the car has been sitting outside, use a 40% range buffer

O **bserve your energy usage**—always try to make sure your 30-mile average projected range is greater than the distance to your destination.

L **imit your speed**—if you are losing your cushion, slow down. Range is VERY dependent on speed.

D **etermine typical consumption**—for a given set of conditions, range is fairly predictable. Pay attention and remember how the car behaves.

All batteries—including the Model S battery—perform worse when they are cold[68]. Model S has a sophisticated heating system to ensure the battery performs at its optimum, but it isn't magical. Keep the following in mind when

---

[68] On a related note, "cold" is the best temperature to store Lithium-ion cells (at approx. 50% charge)

the temperature drops below 50°F (10°C) (and especially when the temperature approaches or is below freezing):

- The apparent range of the battery will be lower than it actually is. As the battery warms up, the apparent range will *increase* until it reaches the "true" (normal operating temperature) range.

- In cold weather you may see a dashed yellow line in the regen part of the power meter, and at the top. A cold battery is incapable of delivering maximum power, or being charged as quickly. Model S limits regenerative braking power until  the battery warms up. The temporary lack of regen can catch owners by surprise.

- Seat heaters use much less power than the cabin heater.

Range can drop by as much as 60% in very cold and snowy conditions. If you are concerned about your range in cold weather, drop the cabin temperature and use the seat heaters instead.

MAXIMIZING RANGE

Quite a few factors affect your range, from your driving habits to the environment, to lights and climate control. Here's a quick summary of how to increase your range:

	Better	Worse
Speed	Low	High
Hills	Downhill	Uphill
Wind	Tailwind	Headwind
Outside Temperature	Hot/Warm	Cold/Freezing
Range Mode	On	Off
Cruise Control	On	Off
Accessories	Off	On
A/C and Heating	Off	On

USE RANGE MODE

Model S has a special "Range Mode" that is accessed via the Settings page on the touch screen. When enabled, it reduces the power of the climate control system to conserve energy.

USING REGEN EFFECTIVELY

As a reminder: "regen" is the recovery or regeneration of energy to recharge the battery when the car goes downhill or slows down. This conversion of kinetic energy (the car's speed) to electrical and ultimately chemical energy in the battery increases your driving range.

To get the most out of regen, it is best to leave the regen setting at "Standard." This provides enough braking force to slow the car down in most situations without using the brakes. You are

therefore capturing as much energy as possible back into the battery. I've only found two circumstances where setting regen to low makes sense—*hypermiling* and on long freeway trips.

Hypermiling[69] is the practice of squeezing every possible yard or meter of range from a battery. For some Model S owners, it's a competition to push the car far beyond its rated range. In fact Elon set the "400 mile" challenge in May 2012.[70] Dave Metcalf and his son were the first to do this, driving 423.5 miles in November 2012.[71] The current (February 2015) record is held by Bruno Bowden, who drove his Model S 425.8 miles non-stop.[72]

Most of us will never try hypermiling, but we will take long trips on freeways. On the freeway it is normal to lift off the accelerator slightly if the car in front changes lanes, or if you need to create a little more distance to the car in front. In this situation the normal regen can be a little aggressive, whereas the low setting allows you to coast. I find the low setting a little more relaxing on the freeway, and it is a little more efficient.

---

[69] A web search on the subject will provide additional information on hypermiling techniques.
[70] http://www.teslamotors.com/blog/model-s-efficiency-and-range
[71] http://www.teslamotors.com/customers/story-david-adam-metcalf
[72] https://twitter.com/brunobowden/status/306847043589132288

A note about regen and hills. Regen in Model S is up to 80% efficient—in other words, if you use 1 kWh to drive up a hill, you'll gain back about 0.8 kWh going down the other side. If you live in a particularly hilly area you might need to take this into account in your range calculations, and it can explain why the same trip in two different directions can yield *very* different energy consumptions.

LONG DISTANCE DRIVING

Model S is the first battery electric vehicle in which you can drive long distances without too much concern. As the Supercharger network continues to be built out this will become even easier. On January 25, 2014 John Glenney (forum member @myfastlady) and his daughter Jill completed the first ever Model S coast-to-coast Supercharger trip, covering 3,600 miles from New York to Los Angeles. Though the Supercharger network is not yet complete, it is still relatively straightforward to drive moderate distances beyond the range of your battery if you do a little planning beforehand using a large array of on-line resources.

@**Doug_G** on the Tesla Motors Club forum has a great list[73] of tips and tricks for long distance driving. It can be summarized simply as "take it easy, plan ahead, and pay attention."

@**ChadS** has a similar take on things.[74]

A team of students and teachers at CPNV in St. Croix, Switzerland has developed a website[75] that will let you calculate electricity usage for a route taking account of elevation changes.

Cliff Hannel (who sadly passed away in 2014) and his son Ben developed a range forecasting/route calculator that uses real world Model S data for accuracy.[76]

---

[73] http://www.teslamotorsclub.com/entry.php/96-The-Rules-of-Model-S-Road-Tripping
[74] http://www.teslamotorsclub.com/showthread.php/13678-How-to-plan-a-road-trip-how-long-will-it-take
[75] http://www.jurassictest.ch/GR/
[76] http://evtripplanner.com

CHARGING ON THE GO

If you need to charge while out and about, make sure you download some or all of the charger station apps for your phone:

- PlugShare—www.plugshare.com
- ChargePoint—www.chargepoint.com
- Blink—www.blinknetwork.com
- CarStations—carstations.com
- Open Charge Map—openchargemap.org

If you want to be able to plug into different outlets, Tesla has a set of adapters for the UMC. But what if you want to plug into an outlet for which there is no adapter? Or you need a longer cable? Check out the Do-It-Yourself guide to adapters[77] (thanks to user @shop on the TM forum).

If you plan to charge at relatives' homes, RV parks, and other outlet sources, you may want to put a non-contact voltage probe, such as the "Triplet Sniff" (available on Amazon.com) in your charge kit. It lets you easily and safely find out if an outlet or wire actually has power, and troubleshoot a large number of issues quickly.

Using driver assist features _____

Traffic-aware Cruise Control (TACC). If using cruise control with TACC enabled, Model S will automatically slow down to maintain a specificed 1-7 car separation if there is a slower car ahead in the same lane. If the car ahead pulls away, or pulls out of the lane, or you change into a clear lane, Model S will automatically accelerate to resume the set cruise control speed.

Novice mistakes for regular driving _____

There are lots of things about the Model S that are different from old technology cars. Whether it's the door handles, or the charge port, or the touchscreen, your first few weeks of driving will lead to a few surprises and maybe a little puzzlement. Here are a few quirks that are worth knowing about.

---

[77] http://cosmacelf.net/Home%20Made%20Adapters.pdf

My passenger can't get into the car. When the car is put into gear the door handles automatically retract and the doors lock.[78] If you stop to pick up a passenger there are two solutions to

extend the handles: put the car in Park (or press the Park button if the car is already in Park), or use the screen controls to unlock the car. The handles will present.

> I usually force the handles to present by pressing the Park button even if the car is already unlocked—many passengers don't realize or forget that they must press the door handle to make it extend.

Mirrors in reverse. With the Tech Package, Model S remembers two separate mirror positions: one for regular driving, and the other when you are in reverse. Many owners complain that the reverse setting doesn't work, i.e., when

they put the car in reverse the mirrors don't automatically change. The trick is that the car *must be in reverse* when you set and save the mirror angle. Put the car in reverse, adjust the mirrors, and hit the save button on the profile drop down.

You'll also need to ensure that you have "Mirror Auto-Tilt" enabled on the Settings page of the touchscreen. After that you should be good to go.

Rear camera disappears. The rear camera automatically comes on when you put the car in reverse, but sometimes it doesn't stay on. If you put the car in reverse then select any control that will put a different display on the touchscreen—say to choose a new radio station—the camera view disappears. To get it back simply press the camera icon, or put the car in park or neutral then back in reverse.

Using the rear view camera when it's raining. Model S is unusual (unique?) in that it lets you drive with the rear camera turned on. Some owners like this;

---

[78] The doors lock if you have "Drive-Away Door Lock" enabled on the Settings screen.

personally I'm not a fan. Regardless, due to the aerodynamics of Model S the camera quickly becomes obscured in the rain. Various owners have tried dabbing products like Rain-X® onto the camera lens to keep it clear, but so far without luck.

Rubbing the "B-pillar" when you enter the car. The B-pillar is the upright part of the body between the front and rear doors. On Model S the B-Pillar is quite wide (to help with roll-over protection) and for some owners (but not all) their shoulders rub against the leather on the B-pillar when getting into and out of the car, causing wear and damage. Be careful.

Riding your brake as you back out of a tight space. There are times when you might want to ride your brake while pressing gently on the accelerator—for example, squeezing a very wide Model S though a narrow garage door opening. Be aware that if you press the accelerator and the brake simultaneously, Model S emits a warning sound. If you do this repeatedly the car will shut down. Instead, turn on "Creep" and use the brake to help you ease out of a tight space without pressing on the accelerator.

Direction of travel on the map. Press the small "direction" icon at the top of the navigation display to switch between "north up", direction of travel or route overview (if you are navigating). Note that you are not limited to pressing the icon itself: pressing anywhere in that part of the display will switch the direction.

Strange noises that are normal for Model S. Every car has a unique audible signature, and the Model S is no different. On start-up and as it moves, the model has emits and unique collection of normal sounds.

> **When you turn the car on you'll hear various clicks and clunks. This is the battery being electrically connected to the rest of the drive train. It's absolutely normal.**

- Under high air conditioning load you'll hear a whining or buzzing noise from the front of the car. This is the A/C compressor.

- Under hard acceleration many owners hear a whine from the drive train. There are many suggestions as to what causes it, but regardless of the cause it seems to be "normal." Excessive noise from the motor should be reported to Tesla Service immediately.

- Some owners have reported a large "thump" when they start moving after the car has been parked for some time. Most likely this is caused by the brake calipers jumping free of the brake disks, and can occur in any type of car if the brakes were wet when the car was parked. This is to be expected and is not a problem.

There are of course, a variety of warning tones and other predictable operational noises. But any other thumps, bumps, whines, or grinding are not normal.

Silent travel and the danger for pedestrians. This has (in my opinion) been over played, though sitting in the Model S one sometimes forgets just how quiet the car is. Although Model S is quiet at very low speeds, above 10-15 mph it makes almost as much noise (mainly from the tires) as any other car. At any speed it is up to you as the driver (as with any ICE car) to be careful around pedestrians.

Rear Facing Child seats. Though a great innovation and generally loved by kids who use them, they are not without a few minor problems.

- There are no A/C ducts (and hence, no direct heating or A/C) in the trunk area. Ventilation fans don't reach the rear facing seats very well, and there is no heat reduction film on the rear window. This can cause problems in very hot climates. Installing film (black limo tint), and/or using small battery-operated fans alleviate the problem. Also, make sure the second row vents are open as wide as possible and pointing up.

- Some owners report that the seats are not comfortable for long trips, but the kids don't seem to mind too much.

- At night the headlights of the cars following your Model S can shine in the kids' eyes.

Lots of little questions

There are dozens of little questions that are addressed in the official *Model S Owner's Manual* but are hard to dig out without some effort. Here are some common questions along with brief answers:

Q. Do my brake lights go on when I take my foot off the accelerator?

A. Yes. The brakes are triggered by regen, but exactly when they come on depends both on the amount of regen and your speed. For example, at 30mph the brake lights come on at about 30 kW of regen.[79] At 10 mph it requires only 10 kW.

> A good rule of thumb is that the brake lights come on when regen in kW is the same as your speed in mph.

Q. What's the best setting for my windshield wipers?

A. Wiper control improved between software versions 4 and 5. I keep the wipers on automatic step one (the first click on the twist control).

Q. Why won't my electronic toll tag/gate pass/radar detector work properly?

A. The Model S windshield contains a metallic film (presumably to reduce heat transfer). Unfortunately, the film blocks signals to/from most devices that transmit a signal. In most cars the area just to the right of the mirror mount base (where it attaches to the glass) does not have the film, so mounting there should work.

I say, "should" because allegedly at least one batch of nearly 2000 windshields was made with no gap in the film. I had to resort to mounting my Florida Toll Tag on the front bumper behind the nose cone.

Q. Can I use navigation if I don't have the Tech Package? (Pre-autopilot cars)

A. Yes and no. Without the Tech Package you will *not* get turn-by-turn instructions, nor will navigation or maps appear in the instrument cluster, and you won't see your route on the touchscreen. But you *can* zoom and

---

[79] As a reminder, the amount of regen is represented as a green dynamic display shown in the lower right had quadrant of your speedometer.

pan the map on the touchscreen with your car location accurately displayed in real-time, you can search for locations by voice or keyboard input, and you can turn on the traffic overlay.

Q. What's the best place to install a radar detector?

A. Due to the metallic film some owners have had problems with radar detectors mounted in the car. As an alternative they can be mounted at the front of the car, but running cables through the firewall can be problematic. The simplest solution is to run the wires across the base of the A-pillar and into the A-pillar trim. A more complex solution is to drill through the firewall in the center of the car where the A/C line enters the cabin. If in doubt, use a professional installer.

Q. What should I put in my glove box?

In addition to the regular items (any registration paperwork that is required in your state/country, and any other critical docs such as an insurance card), make sure you have:

1. This book!
2. Your J1772 adapter; there's a place for it at the back left of the glove box.
3. The *Model S Owner's Manual*.

Q. What should I put in the cubby (under the touchscreen)?

A. That's where I keep a micro-fiber cloth to clean the screen(s). A thick cloth won't trigger the touch sensors and you can clean the screen without invoking the "screen cleaning" special setting.

Q. What should I have in my frunk and/or my rear storage compartment?

1. Tire inflation kit (available in the Tesla online store). Other variants are available at most auto parts stores or on the Web.
2. Cleaning cloths and/or other cleaning materials.
3. I keep a moving blanket in the trunk well that I use to protect the trunk and/or large objects.

Q. How do I leave my car turned on when I'm not in the car?

A. This is one of the most problematic things about Model S. The simplest thing is to simply leave one of the doors or the trunk open (or ajar). If you want the car to be shut but on (e.g., at a drive-in movie) just make sure you are in the driver's seat. If someone is in the passenger seat but not in the driver's seat, it will be necessary for them to press the touchscreen every 30 minutes or so to keep the car on. If you want to leave the car on while you are away from it, follow these steps:

- Sit in the driver's seat with your foot on the brake
- On the controls screen choose "E-Brake and Power Off'
- Use the button to put the car in neutral, and then the button to apply the parking brake.
- Exit the car and manually lock it.

This should leave the car on indefinitely. Remember to turn off the automatic lights and wiper settings, and set the A/C appropriately.

Q. I want to show my car at a local event, but don't want people accidentally moving it. What do I do?

A. Take your UMC cable with you and plug it into the car's charge port. You can hide the other end under the car. The car will refuse to go into gear with the cable connected, even though it is not plugged in.

Q. Why is there a 12V battery?

A. Two main reasons: (1) to power the accessories (e.g., lights, touchscreen, A/C) and (2) to isolate the main battery. All of the Model S accessories use the same 12V circuitry that other cars do, along with many of the same components. Using a regular 12V battery keeps things simple. The main battery is isolated from the rest of the car when not in use for safety reasons. To drive the car it is necessary for a pair of *contactors* to close and make an electrical connection. This is called the HVIL, *or High Voltage Interlock*. The 12V battery powers the interlock. This explains both the clicking you hear when you turn the car on/off and the reason you can't start the car if the 12V battery is dead.

Q. Where is the 12V battery?

A. The 12V battery is on the passenger side of the car in the wheel well behind the front wheel (in older cars), or in the center of the windshield behind the frunk (in newer cars).

Q. What happens if the 12V battery dies?

A. The car won't start. You'll need to jump the car using the 12V posts behind the nose. After it starts you can disconnect the jumper cables. The car will keep running (and potentially charge the 12V battery), but it is best to get it checked out by Tesla Service as soon as possible.

Q. What happens if I flatten the main battery (a.k.a. "bricking")?

A. Under extreme circumstances it is possible to discharge the battery to such a level that it cannot be recharged. It is said to be "bricked." Although claims about bricking created a media firestorm in the early part of 2013, it is nearly impossible to brick a Model S battery under normal circumstances. Testing by owners suggests that the car keeps 3.9 kWh (on an 85 kWh battery) reserved for emergency use (not driving), which seems to agree with the *Model S Owner's Manual*.

> **"Discharging the Battery to 0% may permanently damage the battery. To protect against a complete discharge, Model S enters a low-power consumption mode when the charge level drops to 5%. In this mode, the Battery stops supporting the onboard electronics to slow the discharge rate to approximately 4% per month. Once this low-power consumption mode is active, it is important to plug in Model S within two months to avoid Battery damage."**

In normal use, with Energy Saving mode enabled, Model S loses only 1-2 miles of range per 24 hours if not plugged in, but it is best to keep the car plugged in whenever possible.

11 Interacting with the Model S Displays

The *Model S Owner's Manual* has excellent explanations of the functions and use of the Model S displays, but there are a few tips and hidden items that may not be readily gleaned from the manual.

Terminology

There are two displays in Model S. The larger is the *touchscreen* (also known as the *17-inch display*); the smaller (behind the steering wheel) is the *instrument cluster*.

Dismissing a pop up window

Whenever a pop up window appears (e.g., the A/C controls), you'll see a little (X) in the top corner to dismiss the window. Pressing the "X" can be difficult to do when driving. There's a much easier way:

> To dismiss a pop-up window, simply touch anywhere on the touchscreen outside of the pop-up.

Rebooting the displays—why and how?

Two different systems control the main touchscreen and the instrument cluster. Occasionally, functions may freeze, stop working, or not perform as expected. The simplest solution is often to reboot one or both screens.

> Reboot the touchscreen by pressing, holding for 5 seconds and then releasing both scroll buttons simultaneously.

Sometimes, a reboot can "mysteriously" solve small control problems associated with the interior. For example, after a software update, one Model

S owner reported that his passenger side door would not open. Pressing on the door handle didn't work. Rather than calling service, he rebooted both the touchscreen and the instrument cluster. The door opened normally!

> **Pressing, holding for 5 seconds and releasing the buttons above the scroll wheels, reboots the instrument cluster.**

Voice input

To date, the number of voice commands is relatively limited, but it's likely that the number will grow with future software updates.

With earlier versions of voice control, the most frequent problem was speaking too soon after pressing the "talk" button. With software version 5.8 and later the delay between pressing the "talk" button and the start of recording has been significantly reduced, almost eliminating this problem.

Voice input activation button.

Most owners don't have a problem getting the car to recognize their voices, but a few owners do. As with any voice recognition system, clear, slow pronunciation is the best approach.

Using the steering wheel controls

The controls are relatively straightforward. Pressing and holding either the left or right scroll wheel allows you to select which displays appear in the left and right windows (respectively) of the instrument cluster. The left scroll wheel controls the volume, which famously goes to "11."

Hidden display elements and interactions _____

There are several undocumented display elements.

The Tesla "T."

As discussed elsewhere in this book, pressing the Tesla "T" logo at the top of the touchscreen will pop up an image of the car (accurately reflecting color, options, etc.), the current software version, and a link to the software release notes (the list of what has changed in this software version).

With the car image on screen, if you press and hold the car model logo (S60, S85, P85, etc.) in the bottom right of the window for about 10 seconds, an "Easter egg " will appear showing a picture of the Tesla factory staff.

Pressing and holding the Tesla "T" logo will pop up a code-entry screen that the service engineers use to put the computer into service mode, enabling the display of detailed configuration information and various test screens. The code is not accessible to owners.

But if you have air suspension and enter the code '007', the suspension display on the Controls screen will change to show the Lotus Esprit from the James Bond film "The Spy Who Loved Me". Why? Because Elon owns the prop from the film!

Quirks when you're in D(rive)

You can move the car from Drive to Neutral and back without touching the brake if you are moving above 5 mph. You can move the car from Drive to Reverse (and vice versa) without stopping if you are below about 5 mph.

Quirks when you're in P(ark)

When you put the car in Park, all the interior lights come on. They cannot be turned off by pressing them. You will need to wait for the lights to time out, or go to the Controls screen and turn off "Dome lights."

HomeLink tips

HomeLink is GPS aware—the menu will automatically appear when the car reaches the location where it was programmed. When you program HomeLink, try to place the car where you'd like the menu to trigger. For example, if you have a gate opener to your neighborhood, don't program the car at work!

Software updates

A message will appear on the touchscreen when a software update is available. This means that the car has already downloaded the update, and is ready to do the install. You can choose to install it immediately, schedule it for a particular time, or dismiss the dialog completely. If you choose to install later, pressing the alarm clock icon on the status bar will bring up the dialog box again.

Occasionally when you start the update it will fail. This could be for one of two reasons:

1. The download did not complete successfully. In this instance the only option is to contact Ownership or Tesla Service and they will reinitiate the download.
2. Tesla identified a bug on the update and does not want you to install it. In this case a reboot of the touchscreen will remove the update icon.

Miscellaneous problems

Most quirks (e.g., TuneIn favorites missing, phone contacts not working) can be fixed by a two-thumb reboot of the touchscreen.

12 Other Tips and Tricks

Emergency Situations

Model S is an extremely safe car, but emergencies do happen. The car's sensors provide data that can be used by the software to inform the driver of an emergency situation. This can be something as simple as a flat tire or something as serious as a major drive train fault or a battery failure. Always act immediately if Model S warns you of a problem and follow the directions provided.

> Emergency Brake: When you are moving, pressing and holding the "P" at the end of the gear stalk works the emergency brake. The brake will release as soon as you stop pressing "P."
>
> WARNING: the behavior switches at about 5 mph. Above 5 mph the "P" works the emergency brake and slows the car gently. Below 5 mph the "P" works the parking brake and brings the car to an abrupt halt.

Instruments and Controls

"Dashed yellow lines." Occasionally one or two dashed yellow lines may appear in the power meter on the right hand side of the speedometer. Most owners are confused by these display elements and don't understand what they mean.

The dashed yellow line in the bottom half of the power display. When you max charge, the car temporarily disables regen (the electricity has nowhere to go). The dashed line shows that regen is limited. As you drive the first few miles, the line will get closer to the bottom of the display then disappear.

This same yellow line appears when the battery pack is cold—typically caused by the weather being below 50°F (10°C).

The dashed yellow line in the upper part of the power display. If you absolutely mash the throttle at around 70+mph you'll be pulling greater than 360 kW (460kW in the P85D). If you repeat this you'll eventually see a dashed line appear at the top of the power meter. This indicates that the car has started to limit the maximum available power, most likely due to heat build-up in the battery. The line will disappear after the battery has had a chance to cool down. The same thing happens if the battery is too cold—it can't release its maximum power. Once the battery warms up the line will disappear.

Driving away without the key. Through software version 5.8 it is possible to drive away without a key, and with (initially) with no warning from the car. For example, you can unlock the car, put the key down outside the car, get in and drive away. Everything behaves as normal. With version 5.8 and above, after ¼ of a mile or so the car will warn you that the key is not present, but will keep driving.

> If you get out of the car you will not be able to start it again—even if you unlock it with your smart phone. Several owners have been stranded by this scenario, and have required someone to bring a key to them to get going again.

Accessory Mode. As discussed earlier, if you want the car to remain powered on after you exit, put the car in neutral and then use the E-Brake from the Control screen.

Alarm. One aspect of "working as designed" might surprise some people. If a passenger is seated in the car, and the driver walks away with the key, the car will auto lock AND auto arm the alarm. If the passenger then opens the door the alarm will go off and can only be disabled by unlocking the car with the key (and maybe with the console). You have been warned.

Dead Key. The *Model S Owner's Manual* describes how to get into the car with a dead key (place it against the lower front edge of the passenger windshield). It has been alleged[80] that that you CANNOT start the car if the battery in the key is completely dead, but technical specifications for the key

---

[80] http://www.teslamotors.com/forum/forums/securing-model-s-while-surfing?page=1#comment-186347

from Texas Instruments describe a low frequency resonant circuit that enables the car to communicate with the key even if the key has no battery in it. In a "dead key" situation, place it in the cup holder, or near the USB outlets. This is where the low-frequency transmitter is located.

> Extra tip: Keep a spare CR2032 battery in the car so that you can replace a dead battery in the key in an emergency.

Slacker/TuneIn. You can use your own Slacker and/or TuneIn credentials to get access to your playlists and favorites from other devices. Go to Settings, Apps, Media.

A couple of tips when using Slacker:

- When searching for songs, wait until you see "Recording..." appear in the instument cluster before you start speaking.
- User @riceuguy on the Tesla Motors forum reports that Slacker search on Model S doesn't like apostrophes. Delete them from titles and names before hitting search.

> **Extra tip: If Slacker is not behaving as you'd expect it to, it is possible it is not logged in. Go to Settings → Apps and check.**

Voice Commands:

You can play music directly from Slacker by saying "Play [artist]", "Play [song]" or "Play [song] by [artist]." You can say, "Listen to" instead of "Play."

To navigate using voice commands, say, "Navigate to" or "Where is" followed by an address, a partial address, a city, a company name, or a keyword/category.

To call someone (using a Bluetooth connected phone), say "Call" or "Dial" followed by the person's first and/or last names.

Interior

Seats. If you have leather seats, there's a little pocket at the front of the driver's seat that is perfect for a ChargePoint card or other bits and bobs.

Frunk. The frunk (front trunk) is the storage area that can be accessed by lifting the hood of Model S. The square storage space at the back of the frunk (for rear-wheel drive cars) is called the "microwave." The microwave does not exist for dual-motor cars (the volume is used to house the front motor).

> Despite statements to the contrary, you *can* fit a 19-inch wheel/tire in the frunk of 2-wheel drive cars, though it has been reported that late-2013 cars have a slightly smaller frunk due to relocation of the DC-DC subsystem.

Charging

The act of charging your vehicle, whether at home or on the road, is central to the Model S ownership experience. In this section, we look at a few tips and tricks.

J1772. The SAE J1772-2009 electric charging connector (usually referred to as simply "J1772") was adopted as standard charging equipment for BEVs (e.g., the Nissan Leaf) and plug-in hybrids (e.g., the Chevy Volt) in the United States. Most charging stations in the U.S. make use of J1772. For both aesthetic and engineering[81] reasons Tesla chose to design its own adapter. Tesla therefore provides an adapter to charge Model S at a J1772 compatible charging location.

> There's a space at the back corner of the glove box that is designed to store the J1772 adapter.

Universal Mobile Connector. The UMC is the charging cable and connector that is provided with every Model S. The charger itself is on-board the vehicle, so the UMC is used to provide a link between the wall outlet and your Model S.

> If you're interested in the internals and wiring of the UMC, TMC forum user @TonyWilliams has done a complete tear down.[82]

---

[81] SAE-J1772-2009 covers "Level 2" charging up to 240V and 80A. It does not currently cover Level 3 DC charging, as provided by Superchargers.
[82] http://www.teslamotorsclub.com/showthread.php/16783-Tesla-Model-S-UMC-cut-open-and-modified-to-J1772

Charge Port. The charge port is found under a small hidden door in the left rear taillight. Note that the charging port and the UMC on the North American and European cars are different:

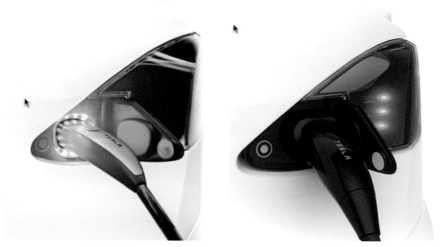

Image © Tesla Motors. Used with permission.

The North American charge port (left) is slightly smaller and the ring around the port lights up. The European port (right) is larger, and the lights are in the light cluster to the right of the port as you look at it.

There are at least four ways to open the charge port:

1. Press "Controls" and use the Charge Port button at the bottom left of the screen.
2. Press the battery icon and there's a button at the top right of the pop up.
3. Press and *hold* the button on the end of the UMC when you are near the port (you might need to move about 10" above the port). I've found that if I wait a couple of seconds between bringing the UMC towards the port and pressing the button the port opens consistently.
4. Last but not least, the port cover can be opened by levering the left edge open with a small plastic tool, or pushing very firmly on the bottom right corner. This pops open the cover that is held closed by a magnet. It will still require one of the three options above to unlock the port itself so that the UMC can be inserted.

Exterior

The exterior design of Model S has very few critics. The words *beautiful, sleek,* and *aerodynamic* occur repeatedly when people and reviewers describe the car. Let's take a quick look at a few tips and tricks for exterior design elements.

Nose cone. It can be tricky to remove the nose cone (to access the 12V pegs or to mount E-ZPass or a radar detector).

You'll need a tool (preferable plastic, ideally an auto molding remover tool). Slip the tool into the top right part of the oval near where it meets the hood and ease it forward. You will be able to pull the nose cone off. The clips are very robust, and there's little chance that you'll break anything. (Note that the nose cone of the original US Signature cars is a slightly different two-piece structure)

One owner has reported being able to pop open the nose cone by pushing down repeatedly on the two chrome strips either side of the frunk lock when the frunk is open. This did not work for me.

Door handles. The quickest way to extend the door handles when sitting in the car is press the Controls button on the touchscreen, then the Unlock button. Pressing "P" on the stalk will also extend the handles.

> **Older cars without the Tech Package: Although the door handles don't auto present, they *do* auto unlock if you have the key in your pocket. Just touch the handle to present; there's no need to click the key to unlock.**

Brakes. The reason there are *two* brake calipers on each rear wheel is that the smaller is the parking/emergency brake; the larger is the "normal" foot controlled brake.

Moving when powered off. If you need to have the car in a state where it is powered off but can still be moved, use the following procedure:

- Put the car in Park, with the car turned on;
- Bring up the controls screen and select the "E-brake and power off" page;
- Select "Tow Mode;"
- The car should now be off and in neutral.

> *Warning:* According to @chrisdl on the TM forum, the parking brake screw drive actuators need electrical power to change state. Hence, when your battery runs out, they remain in the position they were in when power was lost. If the parking brake was on, it stays on. If it was off, it stays off.

Brake lights. The brake lights come on with both foot braking and regenerative braking. If you want to test this, use the rear view camera or the on-screen display (press the battery on the status bar to bring up the charging screen with a live car graphic) to see the brake lights come on.

Electricity Bills

When you are calculating how much electricity the car uses, the following facts are helpful:

- Model S consumes electricity both while driving and while parked.
- Parked: Tesla says the car uses 1% of battery capacity per day when not plugged in. This is called the "vampire load" or "vampire drain." With early software versions the car used a lot more than 1%— closer to 10–15 miles per day when not in use. More recent (5.8 and above) software versions have reduced this load in most cars to 1–3 miles per day (about 0.48 kWh per day).
- Driving: Say you drive 50 miles/day, and you drive at the rated rate of 0.286 kWh/mile, the motor will consume 50 x 0.286 = 14.3 kWh
- The car will therefore consume 14.3 + 0.48 = 14.78 kWh.
- When charging at 240V/40A, about 86% (based on user estimates) of the electricity in your electricity panel ends up in the battery.

- Therefore the total electricity through your meter in a 24 hour period will be 14.78/0.86 = 17.2 kWh.

- Cold weather will cause the car to use more electricity to heat the batteries.

Utility Bills when charging from 110V: Information from the Tesla Charging Page says that to completely fill an 85 kWh battery requires 132 kWh from a 110V/12A source. This means that while 240V/40A charging is roughly 86% efficient, 110V/12A charging is only 64% efficient—and your electricity bills will be that much higher. In very cold climates some owners have found that 110V/12A charging adds no range whatsoever. All the energy goes into heating the batteries.

13 Caring For Your Model S

Cleaning

After spending a not inconsiderable sum on your gorgeous new Model S, please don't go to the local crappy drive through car wash and ruin the exterior finish. I recommend doing a hand-wash and interior clean as often as you can. There are many very good cleaning products on the market, though the three most recommended by forum members are: Meguires[83], Grigot's Garage[84] and Adam's Polishes.[85] [86]

Exterior

Some owners are happy to use "touch-less" car washes, but even these can damage paintwork. There's also the risk that wheel rims—especially the 21-inch rims—might be damaged by the car wash machinery.

> **The preferred washing approach is to use a "two-bucket" hand-wash technique. This approach involves one bucket containing car shampoo, and a second bucket with clean water.**

- Step 1: hose off the entire car with water, starting at the top and finishing with the wheels.
- Step 2: spray the entire car including wheels with shampoo from a hose-mounted sprayer.
- Step 3: use a micro-fiber wash-mitt to wash the upper half of the car, including the windows, using the two-bucket technique.
- Step 4: use a second micro-fiber mitt to wash the lower half of the car, excluding the wheels.
- Step 5: use a wheel brush and the two-bucket technique to clean the wheels.
- Step 6: use a leaf-blower to remove excess water (it is especially useful to get the water from inside the mirrors, and behind the lights).
- Step 7: use detail spray (I use Adam's Detail Spray) or wax to bring the car up to a perfect finish.

---

[83] http://www.meguiars.com/
[84] http://www.griotsgarage.com/
[85] http://www.adamspolishes.com/
[86] I am not affiliated with any of the companies or products suggested in this chapter and receive no compensation from them.

On YouTube you'll find an entertaining four-part video series that teaches you everything you need to know about the 2-bucket approach, including which sprays, shampoos, and sprayers you'll need. Search for "Junkman's 2-Bucket Wash Technique."

This is my hand-washing setup:

- Two Home Depot 5 gallon buckets
- Two grit guard inserts for the buckets
- Gilmour 75QGF4 Foamaster Cleaning Gun
- Mothers Wheel & Wheel Well Long Handled Brush
- Two Griot's Garage 10268 Micro Fiber Wash Mitts
- Two Monster Microfiber Extreme Thickness 16x16 Towels (bought as a 3-pack)
- One Zwipes Microfiber Cleaning Cloth (bought as a 36-Pack)
- Meguiar's Gold Class Car Wash Shampoo and Conditioner
- Armor All 78482 Wheel Protectant—7 oz
- Adam's Detail Spray—New Forumula—16oz
- Meguiar's NXT Generation® Spray Wax—24 oz
- Rain-X® 2-in-1 Glass Cleaner with Rain Repellent—23 oz

Pretty much everything is available from Amazon.com or your local auto parts store.

EXTERIOR GLASS

I use Rain-X® Glass Cleaner with Rain Repellent on all the windows once I've finished with the detail spray.

Interior

Forum user **@OmarSultan** recommends Grigot's Garage Interior Cleaner, Leather Cleaner and Carpet Cleaner.

INTERIOR GLASS

If you install window film treatments, be sure that you do not use Windex™ or similar products because they might damage the film. My installer recommended using rubbing alcohol, which does not affect the film and evaporates without streaking.

14 Model S Maintenance

As I've already stated, with the exception of the drivetrain and the use of aluminum rather than steel in the body, Model S is like any other car. From that perspective it acquires the same wear and tear on the suspension, bodywork, paintwork and accessories as any other car. The electric drivetrain is dramatically different from ICE cars, and both its technical architecture and its behavior (especially regeneration) have significant (positive) implications on maintenance, as does Tesla Motors' policy toward the car's warranty.

One Month After Taking Delivery

There have been a small number of unpleasant stories about 21-inch tires being worn down to the cord after only a few thousand miles, due to incorrect suspension alignment. In addition to the regular maintenance listed below, check your tire wear after one month of operation. Ideally, re-align your wheels.

Daily Maintenance

The *Model S Owner's Manual* is very clear that the best way to maintain your battery in the best of health is to keep your Model S plugged in:

> "Model S has one of the most sophisticated battery systems in the world. The most important way to preserve the Battery is to LEAVE YOUR MODEL S PLUGGED IN when you are not using it. This is particularly important if you are not planning to drive Model S for several weeks. When plugged in, Model S wakes up when needed to automatically maintain a charge level that maximizes the lifetime of the Battery."

Weekly Maintenance

On a weekly basis you should wash the car, top up the washer fluid and check the tire pressures.

Semi-annual (or 6000 mile) Maintenance _____

It is recommended that you rotate the tires every six months or six thousand miles, especially if you have 21-inch wheels.

Annual Maintenance _____

It is recommended that the car receive a full service every 12 months or 12,500 miles (20,000 km), whichever is sooner. Tesla provides fixed-price maintenance, with a multi-year pre-paid, discounted option where allowed by law.

> For Model S, there is no transmission fluid to replace, no engine oil to top off, and no oil filters to replace, so there are relatively few consumables for you to replace or for Tesla to maintain.

The battery is a sealed unit, as is the motor, the charger(s) and inverter.

Further, the use of regenerative braking means that, unless you are a particularly aggressive driver, the brake pads are hardly used. One Roadster owner reported that he needed to replace the brake fluid before he needed to replace the brake pads.

Tesla does exhaustively check all the components of the car during the annual service, and as the car's design and componentry have evolved, Tesla may choose to replace old parts with new, updated versions. Tesla will usually update the car to the latest software version, and ensure that all the subsystem firmware is also updated. They rotate and align the wheels.

Strictly speaking it is not necessary to service the car to maintain the warranty. However it seems foolish not to pay the relatively modest service fee to keep your $70,000–$120,000 car in tip-top shape.

Real-time Monitoring _____

It should also be noted that Model S streams telemetry data back to the factory so that Tesla can proactively monitor for potential problems. This enables them to identify issues before then impact owners, to redesign affected systems, and to proactively update existing cars where appropriate.

15 Almost Perfect, But Not Quite

Like other premium automobile manufacturers, Tesla Motors works very hard to achieve the highest possible quality for every car that it delivers to its customers. But quality defects do occur. Fortunately, fundamental design flaws have been rare and have been quickly addressed, but minor build quality issues do occur even though it is more than three years since the car first rolled off the production line.

Before discussing problems, it's only fair to provide context. As I mentioned earlier in this book, the Model S has received dozen of accolades from independent automotive reviewers. In addition, the fiercely independent product rating magazine, *Consumer Reports,* awarded the Model S with the highest rating (99 out of 100) it has ever given any automobile. This is an amazing car, and I recommend it to anyone and everyone I speak to.

Design Issues

There have been minor criticisms leveled at the design of Model S, and most of them focus on the car's interior. These include the lack of grab handles above the doors, the lack of cup holders in the rear, the unusual positioning of the front cup holders, and the lack of a center console. While some see these as flaws, others see interior minimalism as a benefit.

In Chapter 17, Customizing and Accessorizing, I discuss aftermarket solutions to some of these "issues." Other flaws—such as the lack of powered folding mirrors on early cars—have been addressed by incremental improvements to the design of the car as the years have gone by.

Product Quality Issues

Based on customer reports, Model S is delivered with remarkably few major quality problems and relatively few minor issues. Many can be resolved quickly, and Tesla has set new standards in the industry with its proactive approach, willingness to resolve problems at its own cost without question, and rapid response to issues. However, like all new model cars, Model S has had its share of glitches. Among them:

12V Battery. The most infamous product quality problem relates to a bad batch of 12V batteries. Model S uses a 12V battery mounted behind the passenger-side front wheel well to power the car's electronics and accessories. On early cars a supply chain issue caused Tesla to be supplied with a batch of some 2000 batteries that failed shortly after cars were delivered to owners. Since the car requires a 12V supply to switch the main battery on, these 12V failures completely disabled the cars. Tesla has both reactively and, where it could, proactively replaced these batteries under warranty.

12V failures NOT related to a bad battery. There have been a handful of instances where the car has died because the 12V battery has failed, where the battery itself was good. The cause in most cases was traced back to the "DC-to-DC" system that charges the 12V battery. In all known cases this was fixed under warranty.

UMC Stuck In Charge Port. There have been a handful of reports—including the car driven by AutoWeek[87]—where the UMC became stuck in the Charge Port. There have been at least two causes for this. One was a software problem that caused the UMC to become stuck when the car was fully charged. Briefly switching to a "range charge" to restart the charging process allowed the UMC to be freed. In the case of AutoWeek (and that of another owner in my own city) the port itself physically failed and was replaced under warranty.

Drivetrain. Reports of problems in the main drivetrain (battery, inverter, motor) have been rare. In all cases the components have been replaced under warranty. It is unclear as to whether these were actually product design issues or build quality problems at the factory.

Tire Pressure Monitoring System (TPMS). One of the more common complaints has been related to TPMS. A number of owners have reported TPMS errors—especially erroneous messages that tire pressures are too low. If you see TPMS warnings and your pressures are correct, contact Tesla Service.

---

[87] http://www.autoweek.com/article/20121210/carnews/121219982

Door Handles. There have been occasional reports of door handles failing (not coming out, not going in, not responding to touch) or doors opening on their own. Some problems can be fixed by Tesla Service rebooting or reprogramming the door controller modules, but some are caused by hardware issues. Tesla redesigned the door handles (and possibly changed supplier) in late 2012/early 2013, and will replace handles on request, under warranty.

General Software Bugs

One of the significant benefits of Model S is the ability to get over-the-air software updates. This means that bugs are generally short-lived and fixed without a visit to Service. Bugs do appear from time to time but can usually be worked around. See Chapter 16, for further details on known bugs, and the section on Software versions, bugs and release notes in Chapter 18.

Build Quality Problems

Model S sales remain "supply constrained," meaning that cars are on back-order and Tesla can sell every car the factory can produce, as fast as it can produce it. Consequently the factory is under immense pressure to produce as many cars as possible, as quickly as possible. Owners continue to report problems both at and after delivery, and this *might* be due to rushing cars through production. Here are a few of the most serious ongoing reports:

Excessive Tire Wear. Probably the most common problem reported on P85 models has been excessive tire wear. And by excessive I mean destroying a set of rear tires in less than 5000 miles. After much investigation by several dedicated owners (most especially @lolachampcar) the cause was finally traced to alignment issues. A correctly aligned car can easily do over 15,000 miles on 21-inch tires, even with an "aggressive" driving style.

> **I strongly recommend that all owners ask for an alignment check at delivery, and/or within the first few months of ownership.**

Condensation in the rear lights. A small number of cars have reported a build up of condensation in the rear lights, caused by incorrect or insufficient sealant on the light cluster. This is easily fixed under warranty.

Poor radio reception. This seems to be a build quality issue rather than a design flaw. A number of cars have been identified to have poorly grounded or poorly installed radio antennas, leading to poor or inconsistent radio reception. The cause can be tricky to troubleshoot, but again Tesla fixes this under warranty.

Creaky/Noisy Panoramic Roof. Various problems with the panoramic roof, including noises and black "goop" sticking to the glass have been traced back to a problem with the sealant used around the roof. There is a warranty fix to use a new sealant.

Charge Port Not Opening. This is a common problem. The charge port door is held closed by a magnet. There is a small degree of adjustment on the charge port door that specifies how strongly it is held closed. Service sometimes needs to tweak this adjustment to get the door to open reliably. It also seems to improve over time.

Air Conditioning Compressor Excessively Loud. Several owners reported noisy A/C, which was traced to the A/C line vibrating against either the steering column or a structural member and causing a high-pitched noise. In both situations the line can be slightly rerouted or the fastenings improved to move it away from the offending item.

The Car Fire Controversy—Debunking the Media Coverage ___

One recurrent concern about Battery Electric Vehicles is the supposed risk of fire from the Lithium-ion batteries. The reaction that takes place in Lithium-ion batteries is *exothermic*, meaning that heat is generated. The heat then accelerates the reaction, which in turn generates more heat, leading to *thermal runaway*.

Ever since the widespread adoption of Lithium-ion batteries in computers, cellphones and cameras there have been occasional reports of battery problems, including overheating, fires and even explosions. One of the most high profile Lithium-ion battery problems was the grounding of Boeing's fleet of 787 Dreamliners in January of 2013 following a number of battery thermal runaway events.

It is for these reasons that Tesla Motors went to great lengths during the Roadster and Model S development phases to do everything practicable to prevent thermal runaway. User **@CapitalistOppressor** on the TMC forum has an amazing write up[88] on the details of the patents behind the battery pack, and the incredible ingenuity of Tesla that has massively increased safety while at the same time reducing cost. These patents include:

- A *recessed terminal and enlarged insulating gasket* on the 18650 cell
- A *custom battery cell with a partial dielectric barrier* for improved battery pack mechanical and thermal performance
- *Cell thermal runaway propagation resistance* using dual intumescent material layers

These and other steps detailed in the write-up both protect against thermal runaway starting, and work to stop runaway should it begin. It should also be noted that "thermal runaway" is actually a relatively slow process compared to a gasoline fire (or gasoline explosion!), allowing ample time to exit the vehicle without injury in the very unlikely situation that it should occur.

Despite all of these efforts, in late 2013 the media reported—with a degree of sensationalism that was completely unwarranted—on three Model S car fires that occurred over a period of two months. In every case the fires occurred as a consequence of a high-speed collision with an object of some kind. In every case, the driver was uninjured. And in every case, Model S fires were treated as if car fires were a rare event—which they most certainly are not.

In the United States, there are about 152,000 car fires[89] *every year*, yet because Model S is new and unique, the media did what the media does. The consequence was bad publicity for Tesla, a significant drop in stock price, and a public misperception that the car might be unsafe.

Elon Musk responded immediately in the media and via Twitter, and later the same week posted a blog entry[90] in which he comprehensively explained the circumstances of the first accident, the technical details that led to the fire, and correspondence with the owner of the car involved in the accident. The owner, Robert Carlson wrote: "I am still a big fan of your car and look forward to getting back into one."

---

[88] http://www.teslamotorsclub.com/showthread.php/17456-Amazing-Core-Tesla-Battery-IP-18650-Cell
[89] http://www.nfpa.org/safety-information/for-consumers/vehicles
[90] http://www.teslamotors.com/blog/model-s-fire

Elon summarized the situation by saying "For consumers concerned about fire risk, there should be absolutely zero doubt that it is safer to power a car with a battery than a large tank of highly flammable liquid."

Home Charging Outlet Problems _____

In November 2013 there was a fire in a garage in Irvine, California in which a Model S was parked and charging.[91] It is alleged that the fire was related to the wall socket into which the UMC was plugged, and had nothing to do with the batteries.

Some small number of UMC adapters have overheated and in some cases melted. These issues can often be traced back to loose wires in NEMA 14-50 outlets, or to incorrectly sized wiring. Heat can quickly build up in the outlet and be conducted along the spades of the adapter into the UMC. 40A is a lot of current, and can quickly generate large amounts of heat due to faulty wiring or bad connections. There *have* been occurrences of faulty UMCs, but these have resulted in the car not charging rather than in any overheating or melting.[92]

In response to this episode, Tesla released software version 5.8.4 (1.49.57), which causes the car to "automatically reduce the charging current by 25%...if the Model S onboard charging system detects unexpected fluctuations in the input power to the vehicle."[93]

On January 10, 2014 Tesla issued a press release[94] acknowledging that Model S owners have seen overheating issues when charging via NEMA 14-50 adapters. Even though the adapter did not cause the overheating, Tesla has redesigned the adapter to include a thermal fuse as an additional safety precaution and is sending a new adapter free of charge to existing owners. Yet another example of Tesla's proactive approach.

---

[91] http://www.bloomberg.com/news/2013-12-19/tesla-says-model-s-charger-didn-t-cause-california-garage-fire.html
[92] http://www.teslamotorsclub.com/showthread.php/25444-Melted-Charging-Adapter-Cord
[93] Release notes for 5.8.4
[94] http://www.teslamotors.com/about/press/releases/tesla-provides-customers-upgraded-charging-software-and-adapter

16 Troubleshooting

Now and then every car presents its owner with a problem, and Model S is no exception. In this chapter I give you advice on what to do if problems arise. For some issues, simple troubleshooting can resolve your problem; for others you may need to call Tesla Service.

Worst-case scenario: the car is completely dead. _____

Don't panic! It could be something as simple as a dead 12V battery. Your best action is to use your mobile phone and get help from Tesla Service. If you strongly suspect you have a dead 12V battery, you can "jump start" Model S

by connecting another 12V battery to the posts (shown in the photograph) behind the nose cone.

The two thumb salute. _____

Phone contacts won't sync? TuneIn radio misbehaving? Map problems? It's likely that the main computer needs to be rebooted.

Model S has been described as not so much a car with a computer, but a computer on four wheels. There is a certain truth to that statement because a computer running the Linux operating system controls the 17-inch touchscreen, maps, web browser and many of the cabin systems (e.g., air conditioning).

We all know that computers can and do go wrong, and it is not unknown for Model S to suffer the odd glitch. Things like maps freezing, A/C pulsing on and off, and phone contacts not synching correctly have been known to happen occasionally.

Should any of the display functions, A/C or even door opening mechanisms go wrong, it can often be fixed by rebooting the main computer using the steering wheel scroll buttons.

Reboot the touchscreen using the scroll wheels.

Pressing, holding for five seconds, and then releasing the two scroll buttons will cause the Linux computer and the touchscreen to reboot (restart).

This can be done while driving as the computer does NOT control the steering, brakes or drive train, and although it *does* control the lights, they will be unaffected by a reboot.

Very occasionally it is necessary to restart the instrument cluster.

Reboot the instrument cluster using the upper buttons.

Restarting the instrument cluster can be accomplished by pressing, holding for five seconds, and then releasing the two buttons above the scroll buttons.

Again, this can be done safely while driving but the instrument cluster *will go blank* for several seconds—hiding the speedometer, etc., in the process.

Note that from an owner's perspective there is no such thing as "rebooting the car." There are dozens of computers and modules in Model S that cannot be restarted easily except by Tesla service technicians.

17 Customizing and Accessorizing

Despite (or possibly because of) spending over $100,000 on a Model S, some owners feel the desire to customize or accessorize the car. Some customizations are simple, others more complex. External modifications usually start with new wheels, wraps, or both.

I'll cover wheels and wraps separately in the following sections, but I have to start with what I think is my favorite Model S, owned by **@Viperbrad** on the TMC forum:

Images © Vossen Wheels. Used with permission.

Sporting a wrap by Signature Custom Wraps in Fort Lauderdale, FL and wheels by Vossen of Miami, FL, I think it looks absolutely stunning. Michael Mogilewski at Signature Custom Wraps[95] has done over 30 Model S's, including wrapping, interior LEDs, and blacking out all the chrome. He's even done some software tuning to increase torque. The pictures of Brad's car crop up all over the Internet, and even appeared (briefly) in a segment of the Colbert Report on Comedy Central in the US.

Wheels

One of the most common customizations is a new set of wheels. When I bought my P85 in January 2013, the 21-inch Turbine wheels (which I love!) were included, but now they are a $4,500 option (in North America, with tires). Many owners have therefore chosen to buy the car with the 19-inch wheels (included in the base price) and then add aftermarket 20-, 21- or even 22-inch wheels.

Here are a few selections to give you some ideas.

The Vossens[96] shown on the previous page are VVS-CV1 in Matte Graphite with a Gloss Graphite Lip. Fronts are 22x9; rears are 22x10.5. Vossen was the first company to offer aftermarket wheels for Model S.

Image © Vossen Wheels. Used with permission

[95] @SignatureCustoms on Instagram. Phone: 954-292-1298.
[96] http://www.vossenwheels.com/

Like the Performance Plus, the wheels are *staggered*, meaning that the rears are wider than the fronts. Owners with this set up comment that the wider rear wheels line up better with the rear wheel arches, and give the car a more "planted" feel. One the downside, the lower profile tires can make the ride a little harsher.

If you want to go completely crazy, you can go with 22x10.5" wheels on the front and rear, though you'll need to use a 3mm spacer on the fronts to avoid them rubbing:

Vossen VVS-CV4 22x10.5 "dual concave" wheels. © Vossen Wheels. Used with permission.

Though Vossen was the first, there are now many other alternatives. User **@evodude919** chose the 20-inch TSW Nurburgring.[97]

To quote Sam, "The 20 x 9 front wheel weighs 23.3 lbs. and the 20 x 10 rear wheel weighs about 24.5 lbs. The offset was 35 mm for both. The tires I chose were the Hankook Ventus V12 evo K110 sized 245-40/20 [fronts] and 275-35/20 [rears]. Both tires have about a 27.7-inch diameter

Image © @evodude919. Used with permission.

which is the same as the stock 19-inch Goodyears. The tires are a little heavy, 28 and 30 lbs. respectively but the combined wheel/tire weight (51.3 lbs., 54.4 lbs.) is a little less than the stock wheel/tire combo (57 lbs.)."

---

[97] http://www.tsw.com/alloy_wheels_nurburgring.php

Forum user **@johnmodels** went with very similar wheels to Sam. John's are Falken RT 7m, 20 x 8.5 front and 20 x 10 rear with at 35mm offset. The tires are Falken 457, 245-40/20 fronts and 274-35/20 rears. Together the tires and wheels were $1800 installed. Since the picture was taken John has switched to Continental DW tires. He likes them a bit more and gets better mileage, likely due to the lower rolling resistance. He believes the 20-inch wheels are a good compromise for the look of a 21 and the ride of a 19, and great value for money.

Image © @johnmodels.

Forum user **@dsterdee** (Don Niemi) went with 22-inch Ace Mesh 7 wheels, 255/30 fronts and 275/30 rears. Both sets are 9 inches wide with a 35 offset.

EVannex founder Roger Pressman **(@soflauthor)** decided to complement his Model S with TSportline 21-inch TS117 forged wheels. These 21x9 front and 21x9.5 rear wheels work well with stock Tesla 21-inch tires. Roger tells me that the TSportline rims weigh considerably less than Tesla's OEM 21's. He ordered the wheels in raw aluminum and had them powder-coated locally so he could get the exact wheel look he wanted.

Image © Roger Pressman, Used with permission.

My last example is from another manufacturer, MHT Wheels, Inc. of Rancho Dominguez, California. Rick Pruden at MHT is a Model S owner—in fact this car is his:

Niche Monotec Stüttgart T70 wheels.[98] Front 21x9; rear 21x10.5. Image © MHT Wheels, Inc. Used with permission.

Niche 3 Piece Concourse A320 wheels.[99] Front: 22x8.5, with 245/30zr22 tires; rear: 22x9.5 with 285/30zr22 tires. Image © MHT Wheels, Inc. Used with permission.

I could go on for pages and pages, but probably best if you head over to TMC and check out the many threads[100] on aftermarket wheels.

---

[98] http://www.mhtwheels.com/mht-luxury-alloy-gallery-vehicle.cfm?id=12312
[99] http://www.mhtwheels.com/mht-luxury-alloy-gallery-vehicle.cfm?id=10078
[100] e.g., http://www.teslamotorsclub.com/showthread.php/22070-New-20-quot-Wheels-amp-Tires

Wrapping

As I discussed in Chapter 5, the range of factory colors for Model S is relatively limited. Occasionally other colors do appear: on a recent trip to the factory in Fremont, California I came across this lovely beast:

And VIN 25000 with this burnt orange paint job that rivals **@Viperbrad's** blue car as my favorite:

But these cars with unusual paint colors are rare. Much more common (and much less expensive) is to go down the "wrapping" route—applying a flexible film to the exterior to change the color of the trim and/or the entire car.

J. McCarthy has wrapped most of the chrome on his car, and powder coated his Turbine wheels (semi-gloss, 40%):

Image courtesy of J. McCarthy/SmartShoot.com. Used with permission.

Forum user **@cohast10475** wrapped his entire car and powder coated his 19" wheels:

Image @cohast10475. Used with permission.

Steven Cohen (@mphmd) went "stealth" on his P85+, going with a matte wrap, powder coated wheels and tinted windows:

Image © Steven Cohen. Used with permission.

Possibly the most dramatic transformation was done by Glen Fagin. He bought a *black* Model S, and then decided he'd prefer *satin pearl white*. Time for a wrap:

Image © Glen Fagin—Encino, CA. Used with permission.

The chrome pieces were removed and then painted gloss black with a clear coat finish. The mirrors and rear diffuser were done in carbon fiber.

For those not familiar with the wrapping process, here's a snapshot of **@garcilamd's** car as it was being wrapped in Frozen Grey matte.

@garcilamd's car color was transformed from silver to frozen grey, and as you can see from the pictures, there's not a huge difference in color. But significant color changes are also possible; Brad's blue car (see the beginning of this chapter and images that follow) began as a brown Model S!

Images © Signature Custom Wraps. Used with permission.

Here are three of Signature Custom Wraps' cars together:

Images © Signature Custom Wraps. Used with permission.

Center Console

One of the most talked about items of Model S is something that isn't there: the center console. Some love the uncluttered look; others can't believe that Tesla left the interior "unfinished." Several options are available to you if want to add some structure to the space.

Tesla Motors announced a "drop-in" center console solution in mid-2013 availability in 2014. After numerous delays and quality issues, Tesla now offers the console in black only with installation required by Tesla Service.

For those owners who want something a bit more unique with the ability to customize both trim (veneer) and upholstery colors compatable with Model S, Roger Pressman and the EVannex team have created a very high quality, owner-installable "Center Console Insert" (CCI). The CCI has

EVannex Center Console Insert (CCI).

been purchased by well over 2,000 Model S owners in 46 states and 8 European countries. If you look closely you'll also see EVannex's unique CubbyCap—a trim-matched door that transforms the storage shelf below the 17-inch display into closed storage. You can find the CCI and CubbyCap at evannex.com.

Mounting a Phone

Despite the incredible power of the touchscreen and its smartphone integration, there are still plenty of reasons to mount your phone within view. Forum user **@sinclairhome** recommends the AIRFRAME from Brookstone.[101] A worthwhile alternative is the RAM Mount Universal X-Grip available through Amazon.com

Protecting the Key

Though it looks very cool, the key is easily scratched if left in pockets with other keys.

Pete White (**@pete8314** on TMC) makes a custom protector based on a USB case that he calls "FobPockets."[102] The buttons can easily be pressed without removing the key.

Image © Pete White. Used with permission.

They are available in leather, neoprene, or my favorite–silicone. Many colors are available on his website, another with other small accessories. Tesla recently introduced its own version, available in your local Tesla Service location.

Touchscreen Screen Protector

For a screen protector for the touchscreen (thanks @slevinn), check out http://nushield.com and type Tesla in the drop down. You can also get screen protectors from the FobPockets website.

Roof Rack and Tow Hitch

In order to reduce drag and increase the range of the Model S, it's wise to avoid a roof rack if you can. If you do want to use a rack, Tesla recently added one to the online store, or you can go to the Yakima website and search for a

---

[101] http://t.brookstone.com/airframe-portable-phone-mount
[102] http://www.abstractocean.com/fobpockets/

2012 MS with the panoramic roof. You should also check out the information at TMC.[103]

The *Model S Owner's Manual* specifically states that Model S is *not* designed for towing, but it can be done. The TorkLift Central EcoHitch for bikes and very small trailers is specifically designed for Model S and is invisible after installation.[104]

User **@Pungoteague_Dave** on the TM forum installed one.[105]

Bicycles in Model S

Don't want to use a hitch, but want to take bikes with you? With the rear seats folded down there is plenty of room for a full sized bicycle—or two if you are very careful. My Cervélo road bike fits in there without removing the front wheel. For casual leisure use I took a different route—the Strida folding bike fits into the trunk perfectly. I have two Strida LTs[106] that my wife and I use when we are on road trips.

Front License Plate Mounts

Some people don't like mounting the front license plate on the nose cone. Of the various alternate solutions, using J-bolts to attach to the grill below the nose seems to be the best.[107] [108] Tesla has confirmed that putting the license place in this location will not cause any cooling problems.

Protecting Your Wheels From Curb Rash

Worried about your shiny new 21-inch wheels? There are a number of options for wheel rim protectors available that attach (fairly) unobtrusively to the rims. These include "Alloy Gators"[109] from the UK, RIMBLADES[110], SCUFFS and RIMBANDS, RIM RINGZ,[111] and WHEELBANDS available at evannex.com They cost about $100, and are about $60 to install (or you can install them yourself).

There's a detailed thread[112] over on the Tesla Motors Club forum.

---

[103] http://www.teslamotorsclub.com/showthread.php/19577-Roof-Rails
[104] http://torkliftcentral.com/ecohitch/
[105] http://www.teslamotors.com/forum/forums/hitch-installation-model-s-and-impact-range
[106] http://www.ultimatesportsonline.com/osc/
[107] http://youtu.be/MY1cGllGVWo
[108] http://www.teslamotors.com/forum/forums/front-lic-plate
[109] http://AlloyGator.co.uk
[110] http://www.rimblades.com/
[111] http://www.rimringz.com/
[112] http://www.teslamotorsclub.com/showthread.php/15141-Alloy-Gators-Rim-Protection-(Pics-and-info)

Fitting Infant Car Seats and Booster Seats _____

The rear seat belt clips are flush with the seats. If you need to use child seats, or have trouble plugging in the seat belts you might benefit from a clip extender.

Head on over to Amazon or eBay and search for "Rigid Click-In Seat Belt Extender: 8 inch, Type A, black."

Customizing Your Garage _____

In addition to installing new charging circuits, a number of owners have upgraded their garage interiors for their new Model S. Some have been simply tidy-ups. Others have replaced old benches with new state-of-the-art garage furniture. Yet others have gone down the decorating route.

CHARGING SOLUTIONS

For home charging there are generally four different approaches.

The first is a simple 110V (North America) or Schuko (Europe) outlet. As discussed in chapters 8 and 12, this is the "solution of last resort" due to low efficiencies and long charging times.

A better, and by far the most common, solution is the NEMA 14-50 (North America) or IEC 60309 Blue or Red (Europe) outlet.

The third is a "Level 2" charger, specifically made for electric cars. Model S owners with other BEVs, such as the Nissan Leaf or Mitsubishi i-MiEV, may choose to go down this route. You may also qualify for a free or discounted Level 2 charger from your power utility or local government.

Last, but definitely not least, is the Tesla High Power Wall Connector, giving 80A continuous load and nearly 60 miles per hour of charging.

When it comes to the installation, many owners take the simple route: an off-the-shelf outlet from the local hardware store.

Here is a typical example from forum user **@myl55**. The picture on the right shows the UMC plugged into a NEMA 14-50 outlet installed adjacent to his main electrical panel.

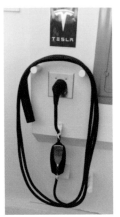

Installation heights for the outlets generally range from 18" to 48" from the floor. Note that the first 20" of the UMC contains the plug and electronics, and although it is robust, it is probably best to keep this off the floor. Marshall has a small clip to keep the UMC controller close to the wall, and has used simple wooden pegs to wrap the cable around.

Image © @myl55. Used with permission.

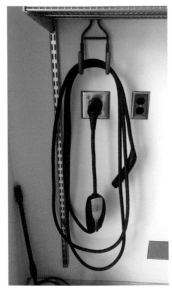

@markb1 went down a similar route. A single NEMA 14-50 socket, flush mounted to the garage wall, with a hook attached to existing shelving.

Tesla designed the UMC to be kept plugged in all the time if desired. When not in use it essentially draws no current, and leaving it plugged in eliminates any wear and tear from the constant plugging and unplugging.

At 20 ft. long it can be a tripping hazard, so it is best if, like Marshall and Mark, you install some kind of hook to keep the cable out of the way when not in use.

Image © @markb1. Used with permission.

If you make the move to an HPWC, installation is very similar to the NEMA 14-50 installs above. The HPWC cable is 25 ft. long, rather than the 20 ft. of the UMC. Evan Fusco, an early Signature owner, did what might be called a "typical" HPWC install—adjacent to his existing panel. Notice that the HPWC cable is a little thicker than the UMC cable, but no less flexible. Also note that at 25 ft. there is plenty of length to reach to the back of the car.

One thing to consider with any installation is the distance from the outlet or mounting point to the charge port on the car. Remember that if you mount the outlet 4 ft. from the floor and run the UMC along the floor, that's 4 ft. of the 20 ft. used up! Also consider whether you'll need to charge your car when it is in the driveway. My electrical panel is at the back of my garage relatively close to the charge port on my car (I reverse in), but I chose to mount the NEMA 14-50 outlet by the garage door so that I could charge outside if necessary.

DECORATING

Some owners keep things relatively simple, whereas others really go to town. Model S owner Brandon Beard managed to track down the exact paint that Tesla uses in its stores: Benjamin Moore 550X Pearl Base—Neon Red, then worked with a local sign company who cut the Tesla logo using a vector file[113] to which he then added the stylized TESLA letters.[114]

Pete White (@pete8314) did a complete refit of his garage and even added a lighted Tesla "T" on the back wall.

---

[113] http://www.brandsoftheworld.com/logo/tesla-4
[114] http://www.brandsoftheworld.com/logo/tesla-motors

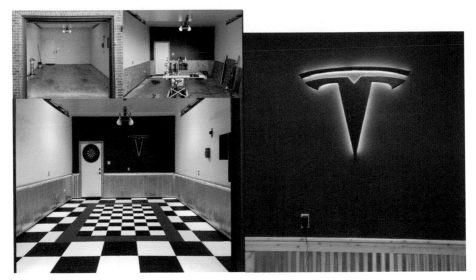

Images © Pete White. Used with permission.

Robert Cotran (@zax123) did something similar. Note that like Evan, Robert mounted his HPWC next to his electrical panel, but also added a NEMA 14-50 outlet:

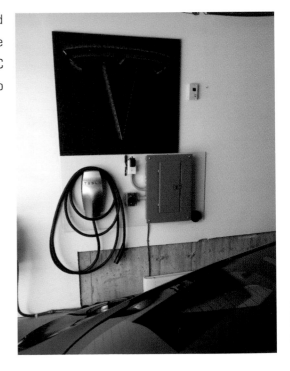

Image © Robert Cotran. Used with permission.

TMC Forum user **@Chris TX** offers a 12-inch by 18-inch replica Tesla Electric Vehicle Parking sign for your garage for only $40. He also has white and red versions that use carbon fiber.[115]

Roger Pressman (**@soflauthor**) and his team at EVannex have created a Cable Caddy that is designed to hang on the wall near your charging outlet. In addition to a hook for hanging your charge cable, it provides you with a place to store all your Model S cleaning products and gear, as well as anything else you'd like to keep behind closed doors. By the way, those closed doors sport a beautiful laser engraved image of the Model S. Visit evannex.com for details.

[115] http://www.teslamotorsclub.com/showthread.php/22738-Supercharger-Parking-Signs-(replica)

OWNING MODEL S

18 Miscellaneous facts, figures, links and info

Videos

MODEL S WALKTHROUGH FOR NEW OWNERS

The official walkthrough of Model S:

http://www.teslamotors.com/models/walkthrough (scroll down the page)

QUALITY ASSURANCE TESTING

A short video of some of the tests Model S goes through at the end of the assembly line: http://youtu.be/YVqlZO7tHFE

BODY, SUSPENSION AND DRIVETRAIN

Peter Rawlinson, ex-VP of Vehicle Engineering at Tesla, walks through the key components of the Model S body, suspension and drivetrain:

- Part 1: http://vimeo.com/18442704
- Part 2: http://vimeo.com/18443539
- Part 3: http://vimeo.com/18443073

FIRST RESPONDERS RIP INTO A MODEL S

A great hour long video about electrical vehicle safety training for first responders, based around Tesla. It covers Model S in some detail, and includes a section where they rip a Model S apart (fascinating but painful to watch):

http://youtu.be/ntK3rvVl2Qw

Model S Service Bulletins

You can find all service bulletins logged with the NHTSA here:

http://www-odi.nhtsa.dot.gov/owners/SearchVehicles

and they are republished on this site:

http://www.ownersite.com/tsb/tsbs.cfm/2013/TESLA/MODEL%20S/

TECHNICAL DETAILS OF MODEL S WHEEL ALIGNMENT

Tesla Service Bulletin SB-13-34-003

http://craigfroehle.com/posted/ModelS_Alignment.pdf

You can also find this information in the on-screen manual accessible via the touchscreen.

Tesla-Oriented Forums and Websites

MODEL S PAGE ON WIKIPEDIA

Presents a reasonably in-depth discussion of the Model S, including sections on its history, production, specification, sales and markets, safety, industry recognition, and media driven controversies.

http://en.wikipedia.org/wiki/Tesla_Model_S

ONLINE FORUMS

The Tesla Motors Club (TMC). The most popular forum for Tesla cognoscenti, it presents many in-depth, long-running topics that are of interest to owners and enthusiasts. Moderated by a team of dedicated volunteers.

http://www.teslamotorsclub.com

The Official Tesla Motors forum. Part of the Tesla Motors website, this forum was designed as a "meeting place" for Tesla owners and enthusiasts. Topics are very current, presented without categorization, and tend to be relatively short-lived.

http://www.teslamotors.com/forums

OTHER SITES

Teslarati. A well-crafted site that presents news, aftermarket product reviews, and rumors for coverage of all things Tesla.

http://www.teslarati.com/

TeslaTap. A site covering Model S features, modifications, and other useful stuff.

http://teslatap.com

Seeking Alpha. For an excellent overview of Tesla's business model and potential future, I'd recommend a very comprehensive, fact-based write up on the site *Seeking Alpha.*[116]

Third-Party Applications that interact with Model S _____

[Warning: technospeak ahead!] Though Tesla has not released an official API, there are various apps that have been created by reverse engineering the iPhone app REST communications. Here are a few:

- Tripography—A web application that records your daily driving distances and shows them in graph form. (http://tripography.com/)

- Visible Tesla—A Java app that runs locally on Mac or PC (or any java-runtime client) that shows similar information to the iPhone app, plus much more detailed charging information.
  (http://www.VisibleTesla.com)[117]

- EVTripPlanner—a web app to capture and report data, and route via charging stations. See http://evtripplanner.com/tracker_about.php

If you are interested in programming and grabbing data from your Model S, check out http://www.teslamotorsclub.com/showthread.php/13410-Model-S-REST-API

Decoding your VIN _____

Here's how to **decode your VIN.**[118] Note that VINs represent the car as it was originally specified; some early cars did not have Supercharger capability but were retrofitted; for those, Digit 7 will be A rather than C:

- *Digits 1–3,* World Manufacturer Identifier (WMI): 5YJ = Tesla
- *Digit 4,* Line/Series: S = Model S
- *Digit 5,* Body Type: A = 5 Door Hatchback LHD RWD
- *Digit 6,* Restraint System:
    - 1 = Manual Type 2 USA Seat Belts, Dual Front Airbags, Front/Rear Side Airbags, Knee Airbags
    - 2 = Euro cars—no details yet.[119]

---

[116] http://seekingalpha.com/article/1463661-on-elon-musk-and-tesla-motors-the-art-of-modern-warfare-in-a-noble-cause
[117] http://www.teslamotorsclub.com/showthread.php/19975-VisibleTesla
[118] This was originally published at TMC. See: http://www.teslamotorsclub.com/showthread.php/7638-Decoding-Tesla-Model-S-VINs
[119] Tesla has not released an updated version of this chart.

- *Digit 7*, Charger Type:
  - A = 10kw Charger
  - B = 20kw Charger
  - C = 10kw Charger, w/DC Fast Charge (Supercharger hardware)
  - D = 20kw Charger, w/DC Fast Charge (Supercharger hardware)
- *Digit 8*, Motor/Drive Unit & Battery Type: [120]
  - C = Base A/C Motor, Tier 2 Battery (31–40kWh)
  - G = Base A/C Motor, Tier 4 Battery (51–60 kWh)
  - N = Base A/C Motor, Tier 7 Battery (81–90 kWh)
  - P = Performance A/C Motor, Tier 7 Battery (81–90 kWh)
- *Digit 9*, Check Digit: Variable
- *Digit 10*, Model Year: [121]
  - C = 2012
  - D = 2013
  - E = 2014
  - F = 2015
- *Digit 11*, Manufacture Location:
  - F = Fremont, CA (FRE)
  - P = Palo Alto, CA (PAO)
- *Digit 12*, Production Series: (for sequence numbers <100,000)
  - A = Alpha Prototype
  - B = Beta Prototype
  - R = Release Candidate Vehicle
  - P = Production Vehicle
  - S = Signature Series Vehicle
  - F = Founder Series Vehicle
- *Digits 13–17*, Production Sequence Number (or Digits 12-17 for sequence numbers ≥ 100,000)

---

[120] Some European owners have reported other letters in Digit 8, but as yet it has not been determined what they correspond to.
[121] Tesla uses the actual year the vehicle was manufactured, rather than the typical US approach of a "model year" that is often ahead of the manufacture year.

Software versions, bugs and release notes_____

Underpinning the driver interactions with Model S is the software that controls the touchscreen, instrument cluster and many of the car's functions. Regularly updated by Tesla and pushed to the car over 3G or Wi-Fi, it is one of the unique aspects of Model S.

Typical to the Information Technology industry, the software has a *version number* that can be seen by pressing the Tesla "T" logo in the status bar of the touchscreen.

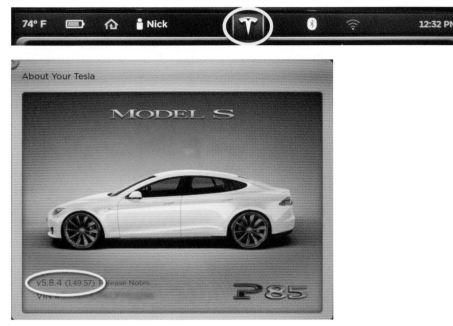

About Your Tesla screen on the touchscreen.

Not all users receive new versions at the same time, and in some cases do not receive them at all. The rollout of new software versions seems— depending on your point of view—a careful approach by Tesla to deploy and evaluate new features and fixes; utterly random; or perverse.

Tesla software has what I call an *external* version number (5.8.4 in the picture above) and an *internal* version number (1.49.57 in the picture).

The first two numbers in an external version (e.g., 5.8) are paired with the first two numbers in the internal version (1.45). Software version 4.5 was internal version 1.33, and 4.2 was 1.19.

A change in version number—say from 5.6 to 5.8—signifies the introduction of new features. These are documented in the *Release Notes*, available in the car from the link shown in the picture above, or on the Tesla web site.

For any given major release (5.8) there can be multiple minor releases (1.49.22, .24, .29 and .30). These minor releases may only apply to specific car configurations (e.g., 70 kWh cars but not 85 kWh cars), to some other subset of cars, or may apply to all cars. Some are only loaded during a service visit, whereas others are pushed to all cars over the air.

Regardless of how many minor releases there are, and how widely they are made available, generally they do not introduce new features and instead are "bug fix" releases to correct glitches in the software. At the time of writing Tesla has yet to produce release notes detailing which bugs have been fixed, nor which bugs are known to exist. 5.8.4 was an exception in that it introduced a new feature—auto-current reduction. (See Home Charging Outlet Problems on page 148.)

Other Miscellaneous Facts and Figures

Slits in back of rear seats. These are not a manufacturing defect. They are tether LATCH anchors for mounting forward facing child seats in the rear seats.

The electric motor. This compact marvel is an AC induction motor rated at 375V capable of 16,000 rpm. It drives the wheels via a 9.73:1 reduction gear.

Alternate Tires. Various users on TMC have suggested the Hankook Ventus as an alternative to the Continentals. You can get a set of four at TireRack for $724 (vs. $1,152 for the Conti's). **@Viperbrad** just put Lexani low profile tires on his car for only $100 each!

NHTSA Crash Ratings. The US National Highway Traffic Safety Administration published their test results at the beginning of August 2013. Model S earned 5 stars in all categories, plus the lowest roll over risk of any vehicle ever tested. Check them out on the NTHSA Web Site Model S page.[122]

---

[122] http://www.safercar.gov/Vehicle+Shoppers/5-Star+Safety+Ratings/2011-Newer+Vehicles/Vehicle-Detail?vehicleId=7769

19 Superchargers

Figure 4 Port St Lucie Supercharger Opening, July 2013.

Introduction

Supercharger stations are Tesla's answer to the "range anxiety" problem I descibed in Chapters 2 and 4. The basic concept behind the Supercharger is simple: charge quickly.

A typical J1772 public charging station will provide roughly 10 miles of range for every 30 minutes of charging. An outlet in your garage can provide 15 miles of range in 30 minutes. A Supercharger? 200 miles!

In a relatively short time, and with still a relatively small number of Model S cars on the road, Superchargers have become incredibly successful. By July 2015, Superchargers had delivered over 44,700,000,000 Wh (44.7 GWh) of energy enabling Model S owners to drive over 153 million miles, avoiding 7,000,000 gallons of gasoline.[123]

How they work

As we've discussed previously, electricity from the grid is delivered as alternating current (AC) but the Model S battery requires direct current (DC). Something (a rectifier) needs to sit between the grid and the battery to convert one to the other. For home and third party public charging this AC-to-DC conversion is done by the Model S on-board charger(s). AC current at the charge port is converted to DC for the battery by the charger.

Superchargers deliver high voltage, high current DC electricity directly to the Model S battery, bypassing the on-board charger. This allows the

---

[123] Information from the display in the Tesla HQ in Palo Alto, CA.

Supercharger to push electricity into the battery as fast as the battery can take it—typically ten times faster than home charging.

But Superchargers are supplied by the same grid that supplies your home, and the grid is AC. So how does the Supercharger provide DC to the car? It does it using exactly the same technology as the Model S charger. In fact Superchargers use *exactly the same* chargers that are in Model S—except instead of using one or two chargers, a Supercharger has groups of 10 or 12.

Grid power is fed into banks of 12 chargers that then feed Model S. Each charger can handle 10 kW, so a dozen provides up to 120 kW. Simple and very, very effective.

When Superchargers were first introduced in California they were rated at 90 kW. Starting in early 2013 new Superchargers were rated at 120 kW, and the original units were retrofitted to bring them up to 120 kW. Initial European Superchargers were rated at 120 kW and are being upgraded 135 kW. Elon has tweeted that North America will also be upgraded to 135 kW, and it is believed that Tesla is exploring pushing the units to 150 kW in the future, further reducing charging times.

For those of a technical bent, here's how a typical Supercharger (in this case, the one at Port St Lucie, FL) is configured: the eight bay setup, like the one shown in Figure 4, takes a 12 kV, 750 kVA feed from the Utility, steps it down to 480V three phase on site, pushes that into 2000A switchgear which feeds four banks of Supercharger (SC) units (one for each pair of "pods") at 480V/200A. Each unit contains twelve 10 kW rectifiers (the same "charger" that is found in Model S) giving a total of 120 kW per pair of pods.

Tips When Using Superchargers

One quirk of the setup is that each bank of 12 chargers feeds two "pods"— the rectangular station that contains the thick Supercharger cable. So two cars connected to the same bank of chargers will share the available 120 kW. Depending on the state-of-charge of each car they may receive 30, 60 or 90 kW, with the other car receiving the remainder. Each pod should have a label on it that shows which bank of chargers (1, 2, 3, 4) it is connected to, and which one of the pair of pods it is (A, B)

So...if you come into a Supercharger station and there are several empty bays you'll need to figure out the best one to use.

> **When you visit a Supercharger, try not to use a pod *number* that someone else is already using. So, if pods 1A, 1B and 2A are in use, do not use 2B. Instead connect to 3A or 3B.**

If there are no labels, then count off the pairs. Unfortunately this approach doesn't always work because some pods are ordered 1A, 1B, 2A, 2B..., whereas others are ordered 1A, 2A, 3A, 4A, 1B, 2B...

As a side note, due to the very high voltages and currents used, for safety reasons the pod that the car plugs into is not energized until the cable has done a "handshake", so that if something crashes into a pod or the cable is cut there is no danger.

The Charging Curve

A 120 kW Supercharger, running for one hour will deliver 120 kWh. If you have an 85 kWh battery, then that means you can go from completely empty to completely full in (85/120) = 0.71 hours, or 43 minutes. Correct? Well— *no.*

When charging Model S at a Supercharger you'll notice that it takes almost as long to fill the last 20% of the battery as it does to fill the first 80%. Why is that?

Think of your battery as a bucket you are filling with water. If you wanted to fill the bucket to the rim, but not spill any, what would you do? When the bucket is empty you

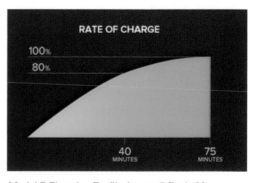

Model S Charging Profile. Image © Tesla Motors. Used with permission.

can run the hose pretty fast, but when the bucket is nearly full you need to slowly close the tap and slow the water down, until right at the very end you drip the last few drops in.

That's exactly what happens as the Supercharger fills the battery. And it's the same thing happens when you charge at home, but since your home charger is nowhere near as powerful as the Supercharger, the difference in speed from start to finish isn't as great, so isn't as noticeable.

> To minimize your time at the Supercharger, make sure that you arrive with a relatively empty battery and try to only fill to 80 or 90%—that way you'll ensure the fastest charging.

For Free, Forever, On Sunlight

When Superchargers were announced, Elon coined the phase, "For free, forever, on sunlight," to describe the experience that owners would have when charging there. The latter referred to solar panels that would be placed on the Superchargers and over the course of a year would generate more power than the Superchargers would use to charge cars.

Supercharger with solar panels and signage. Image © Tesla Motors. Used with permission.

During 2013, Supercharger installation fell behind schedule, so to accelerate the build-out, Superchargers are being built without solar panels and without the "spaceship" signage (the structure in the left of the picture, above). The panels and signage are both over 10' tall and therefore have additional zoning restrictions that delay the permitting process. Tesla is committed to rapidly building the Supercharger infrastructure across North America and Europe, and is currently limited by the local permitting process. They are, therefore, doing everything possible to speed up that part of the process. At some point in the future when some unspecified criteria are met, Tesla will begin the process to add solar and signage to the Superchargers.

20 Battery Chemistry and other techie stuff

Volts, Amps and all that electrical jargon _____

If volts, amps, current, and kWh don't mean much to you, hopefully I can help.[124]

The best explanation I've seen is to use water as a metaphor for what happens when charging or driving Model S.

THE BATTERY

Think of the battery as a bucket. It can be full, empty or somewhere in between. Charging the car is like filling the bucket, and driving the car is like slowly emptying the bucket.

VOLTS AND AMPS

Volts are how we measure Voltage. Voltage is like water pressure. If water pressure is high, water will shoot out of a hose at great speed. Likewise the higher the voltage the faster electricity will flow.

Amps are how we measure Current. Current is the equivalent of the volume flow of the water coming out of the hose.

When you charge the car, the display helpfully (or obtusely, depending on your point of view) tells you how many volts (V) and amps (A) the battery is using (consuming). We use these same measures to describe electrical outlets (e.g., 220 V, 50 A).

KILOWATTS (KW)

Kilowatts, abbreviated to kW, are simply a measure of how quickly you fill or empty the bucket. A car charging at 10 kW will fill more slowly than a car charging at 20 kW. Kilowatts are a measure of "power." Power is actually measured in Watts, but since the numbers we deal with are large we tend to use kilowatts. One kilowatt is one thousand watts.

---

[124] For simplicity I'm going to ignore the various (in)efficiencies inherent in the charging system.

For Model S, voltage will typically range from 110V to 400V. Current will typically range from 12A to 300A.

A 220V, 40A circuit (8.8kW) will charge the car 7 times as fast as a 110V, 12A (1.32kW) circuit. A 400V, 300A Supercharger circuit (120kW) will charge the car 90 times as fast!

KILOWATT-HOURS (KWH)

Kilowatt-hours, abbreviated to kWh, are a measure of how big the bucket is, or how full it is. "I have an 85 kWh battery," indicates the size of your battery. A 70kWh battery is smaller than an 85kWh battery. Kilowatt-hours are a measure of "energy."

Lithium-ion batteries and battery packs

The Model S battery pack is a marvel of engineering. The 85 kWh models pack approximately 7100 individual cells into a 107-inch x 54-inch x 4.5-inch pack that forms the floor of the car.

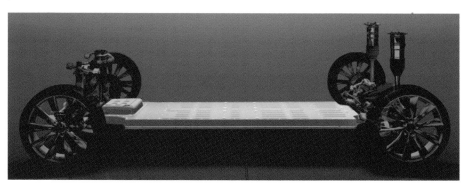

Model S battery pack. Image © Tesla Motors.

Tesla has been somewhat close-mouthed on the details of the battery pack, but there is evidence that the cells are arranged in groups, and the groups are arranged in modules. The 85 and 90kWh batteries may have 16 modules, and the 60 and 70kWh batteries 14. Each module contains six groups.

It is believed that Model S uses a Panasonic nickel cobalt aluminum (LiNiCoAlO2) cell custom-designed by Tesla and Panasonic for 3000 cycles with minimal degradation in capacity. The battery is characterized by superior energy and power densities when compared with common, commercially available alternatives.

90 kWh Pack (can I upgrade?) _____

In July 2015 Tesla introduced the 90 kWh traction pack. Many owners immediately asked if it was possible to upgrade an existing car to the new larger battery. The answer is "yes, but..."

First a word about the battery itself: as I discussed elsewhere in the book, Tesla continuously updates the car—making something like 20 changes every week on the production line. The battery is no different. In the press call that accompanied the announcement, Elon highlights that the new 90 kWh battery now uses silicon in the anode, squeezing more energy into the same volume. At the same time, Tesla changed the huge (in energy terms) fuses that protect the drive train (and the driver!) in the very unlikely event of a serious problem with the battery. The old fuses were rated at 1300 amps and work just like household fuses—they get hot, melt and break the circuit. The new fuses (the secret to Ludicrous mode) are rated at 1500 amps, are microprocessor controlled and can actively disconnect the pack in the event of a problem.

So—can you upgrade from a smaller battery to a 90 kWh battery? Technically yes, but practically no. On the same call Elon said that whilst it is technically possible to upgrade the battery, economically it would not make sense for an owner to do so, and given that battery capacities are increasing at roughly 5% per year it would make more sense to wait a few years before trading up.

Tesla does NOT offer upgrades at this time, and no pricing is available.

Rated vs. Ideal vs. Typical vs. Projected Range _____

As I've mentioned a number of times in this book, range calculations are probably the most discussed aspect of owning Model S. Tesla does not help the situation by having at least four different versions of "Range."

IDEAL = TYPICAL

When Tesla first announced Model S the goal was to have a 300-mile range. Tesla achieved this and the car was sold as such. In May of 2012 Tesla released this graph via a blog entry on their website[125]:

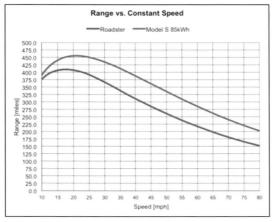

It suggested that Model S could achieve something over 300 miles at between 55 and 60 mph. Tesla subsequently clarified this to be "300 miles at 55 mph on 19-inch wheels on level ground with no head- or tail-wind with no accessories."

Image © Tesla Motors. Used with Permission.

Sometime during the 4.x series of software versions, Tesla formally named this as the "Ideal" range in the user interface. When the car started delivery in Europe, software version 5.0 (available only in Europe at the time) identified this as "Typical" range. These two terms are current at the time of writing this book and are equivalent.

RATED RANGE

As I discussed in Chapter 10, rated range is directly equivalent to the EPA and UNECE test results in North America and Europe respectively. A weird consequence of the different testing results and Tesla's naming convention is that Rated Range in North America is *not* the same as Rated Range in Europe. Although Ideal Range and Typical Range are identical, Rated Range is less than Ideal range in North America (265 vs. 300), but greater than Typical Range in Europe (311 vs. 300).

---

[125] http://www.teslamotors.com/blog/model-s-efficiency-and-range

PROJECTED RANGE

Projected range varies every few seconds and is dependent on your energy usage over the previous 30, 15, 5 or 0.1 miles. Projected range can be found on the energy graph on the touchscreen.

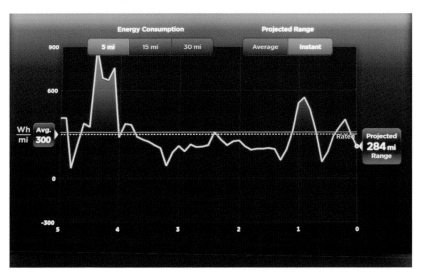

Energy graph from the touchscreen.

If the Projected Range button is set to "Average", then the value on the right hand side of the display will show the remaining range based on the average Wh/m over the last 5, 15 or 30 miles. If the Projected Range button is set to Instant, the value is based on the average consumption over the last one-tenth of a mile.

Battery Pack capacity—what's really available? _____

@RodAndBarbara on the TM forum seem to have gotten to the bottom of the battery/range situation in the 85 kWh car.[126] Here's what they found. It is a bit weird, so stick with me here:

- Let's assume the battery really is 85 kWh

- Tesla has told us that 5% is reserved for system use to avoid "bricking" the battery. Testing suggests that it is actually 3.9 kWh—leaving 81.1 kWh.

- The EPA 265 mile range is based on this 81.1kWh capacity

[126] http://www.teslamotors.com/forum/forums/important-new-information-about-rated-miles-and-projected-miles

- Real-world experience has shown that when the range reads "zero miles" there are still about 17 miles of capacity left (to get you somewhere safe in an emergency); the EPA 265 miles includes these 17 miles.

- 265 miles from 81.1 kWh is 306 Wh/mile. This figure has been known for a long time and is what we've been using to calculate "rated range." This value is shown as a horizontal line on the energy graph and labeled "Rated."

- But ... it turns out this is wrong. The 17 mile emergency reserve means there are 5.2 kWh held in reserve (but available). When "fully charged" on a range charge the display shows 265 rated miles, but the display drops to zero when there is still 17 miles of capacity. Therefore the "rated range" in the car is based on 265 miles from 75.9 kWh (81.1 minus 5.2), therefore 286 Wh/m.

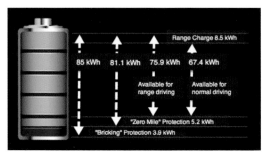

Possible Battery Use Profile.

If you want to get your real range to match rated range as displayed in the car, you need to average 286 Wh/m. But when you get to zero, you've still got 17 miles at 306 Wh/m (or just over 18 at 286).

Why is the dashed line on the energy graph at 306 rather than 286? I have no idea.

The net-net is this:

> The usable capacity of an 85 kWh battery during range-charge, non-emergency driving is 75.9 kWh, and 67.4 kWh for a normal charge. If you divide that by your Wh/m consumption you should get an accurate estimation of range.

I have got a lifetime average 340 Wh/m so at that rate I would get 223 miles from a range charge. YMMV.[127]

---

[127] Your Mileage May Vary.

It is important to note that this information has <u>not</u> been officially confirmed by Tesla and *may be wrong*, but it does agree with everything many users have seen in the last three years. The 15–17 mile "reserve" was confirmed during the infamous "Broder Incident"[128] in which a *New York Times* reporter incorrectly portrayed the Model S as lacking the range to make a Boston to New York trip, and deliberately ran the car until the battery was completely empty.

It is possible that the battery in the 85 kWh cars is not, in fact, 85 kWh but is something larger—e.g., the owner-usable capacity might be 85 kWh and the bricking protection may be additional. We'll have to wait for the official word from Tesla.

---

[128] http://www.teslamotors.com/blog/most-peculiar-test-drive-follow

21 In Closing

It's funny how history has a way of doubling back on itself. Consider the following comment:

> "The electric [car] of today...is a practical, economical and efficient motor car, capable of performing fully 95 per cent of the demands made upon the gasoline car—but the possibilities of that little 5 per cent, though hardly relevant, sell 1,000,000 gasoline cars a year."

So wrote E.P.Chalfont in 1916. That "5%" has meant that for more than 100 years gasoline and diesel vehicles have dominated transportation worldwide. I am absolutely convinced that domination is about to end, and Elon Musk and Tesla Motors are the going to end it.

Time and time again people have sounded the death knell for Tesla. Yet in 2013—the first full calendar year of production for their first car designed from scratch and built in a brand new state-of-the-art factory with a brand new workforce—Tesla generated revenues of over $2 billion and earned accolades from across the motoring world. In 2014 revenues grew by nearly 60% to over $3.5 billion, and Tesla is forecasting to deliver over 50,000 cars in 2015, up nearly 75% over 2014.

Model S threw out the rulebook on what an electric car could be, and in doing so has written a new future for the global automobile industry. The *2013 Motor Trend Car of the Year* is an engineering and design marvel—arguably the most economical, most highly performing, most spacious, and safest sedan on the market. Yet this is just the beginning.

In writing this book my goal was not to try to convince you to buy (or at least consider) Model S as your next car. Instead, I hoped to convince you that the question you should ask is, "Why *wouldn't* I buy Model S?"

I took delivery of my *Performance 85* Model S in January 2013. VIN number 02298 rolled off the production line in Fremont, California in December 2012, and since then I have driven over 20,000 smooth, silent, and emission-free miles, and spent a grand total of $600 on electricity. Doing 0 to 60 in just over 4 seconds, yet with fuel economy of 90 miles per gallon equivalent, my Model S has the performance of a Lamborghini, the luggage capacity of an SUV, the fuel economy of a small motorcycle, and the crash protection of an Abrams tank.

It does 265 real-world miles on a single charge from a regular electrical outlet in my garage, and will recharge in a matter of hours. And if I want to go further? I use Tesla's Superchargers: high performance charging stations that give me 200 miles of range in 30 minutes—for free.

What does the future hold? As Model S continues to improve month-by-month, Model X is about to start shipping, and Tesla is busy building the production line in the massive Fremont factory for its high-volume car, Model 3, that is scheduled for release in 2017.

Superchargers now connect Miami to New York to LA and Seattle via an electric superhighway. Tesla is blanketing the Americas, Europe, China and Australasia with the world's best charging network.

Nearly 3 years in, Model S is still supply constrained—Tesla can't build enough of them to meet demand. The constraint is in the availability of Lithium-ion batteries—so Tesla is building the biggest battery factory in the world. Well, why not?

Elon Musk is systematically executing one of the most ambitious and audacious projects ever undertaken—to move beyond 130 years of dependence on a mine-and-burn hydrocarbon transportation economy to a solar-powered future.

In doing so he has proven to Ford, BMW, Mercedes, Toyota and all the other automotive behemoths that not only can electric power sell vehicles, but that those vehicles can be the best in the world.

The future is here. Welcome aboard.

22 Glossary

18650

A type of Lithium-ion battery cell, named after its size: roughly 18mm diameter by 65mm long.

Battery Swap

In 2013 Tesla Motors demonstrated the ability to remove and replace the Model S battery in approximately 90 seconds. They indicated that they would pilot this technology with a view to putting it into production.

Bricking

When Lithium-ion batteries are completely depleted they can suffer irreparable damage to the chemicals rendering them unable to be recharged. Such a battery is said to be "bricked" because it is as much use as a brick.

CCI

The Center Console Insert, an aftermarket console from EVannex.

CHAdeMO

Originating in Japan, it is the trade name of a quick charging method for battery electric vehicles. The name is a pun for "O cha demo ikaga desuka" in Japanese, meaning, "Let's have some tea," referring to the time it takes to charge the car. It delivers up to 62.5 kW of high-voltage direct current via a special electrical connector. A CHAdeMO adapter for the UMC is "coming soon" in the Tesla online store.

Charge Port

The port on the rear left side of Model S into which the charging cable (UMC) is inserted.

Charger

Generic name for any device that supplies power to Model S, and especially the device in the car that converts AC electricity from the charge port to DC electricity for the battery—strictly speaking a rectifier.

Creep

The software controlled function that mimics the behavior of automatic transmission cars that "creep" forward at low revs due to drag in the torque converter.

Delivery Specialist

Towards the end of the production process you will be assigned a contact person, *the Delivery Specialist*, who will work with you on the details of the delivery and the final paperwork. They should be available to walk you through the car when it is delivered.

Frunk

The "front trunk", under the hood.

HPWC

The *High Power Wall Connector*. This permanently installed, wall-mounted device provides up to 80A of current to Model S when charging at home. It forms part of the *High Power Home Charging Option* (together with the optional 2nd charger in the car).

Inverter

The device in the car that converts DC electricity from the battery to three-phase AC electricity for the motor. Also called the *Power Electronics Module* in Roadster.

J1772

Officially SAE J1772-2009, it is a North American standard for electrical connectors for electric vehicles maintained by the Society of Automotive Engineers. Most non-Tesla public charging stations conform to J1772.

kWh

Abbreviation for Kilowatt-hour. A measure of energy. Typically used to describe battery capacity, battery charge level, or amount of charge desired or received when charging.

Lithium-ion

Descriptive name of the type of rechargeable battery used in Model S. The name reflects the chemical makeup of the battery contents— specifically the positively charged ion of the metal Lithium, generated during the chemical reaction.

NEMA 14-50

The *National Electrical Manufacturers Association* 14-50 Connector is a 50 Amp, 3 wire, single-phase earthing connector, often used for electric cooking ranges and ovens, and for the main heating element of clothes dryers. It has become the preferred connector for home charging in North America for Model S.

OTA

Over-the-air. Used to describe the ability of the car to receive software updates over the car's 3G and Wi-Fi data connections.

Regen—regenerative braking

The act of recharging the battery using current generated from the motor when it acts as an electrical generator when slowing down or going downhill.

Supercharger

Tesla Motors' high speed charging station. A Supercharger consists of two to eight or more bays supplying direct current at up to 400 V and 400 A.

TACC

Traffic-Aware Cruise Control – Tesla's name for what other car manufacturers call adaptive cruise control. Automatically adjusts the car's speed based on the car in front.

Traction Battery

The main battery in the floor of Model S containing Lithium-ion cells. It is the source of motive power for the car, supplying current via the inverter to the motor.

Trunk Well

The space below the trunk. Rear facing child seats fold down into this area when not in use; it is usable space for cars without rear facing seats.

UMC

The *Universal Mobile Connector*. The cable and electronics used to connect the car's charging port to the wall outlet.

Wh/m

Watt-hours per mile. A measure of energy consumption per unit distance. The most common method of comparing one owner's energy consumption to another, and to Tesla's stated performance.

23 Index

About the author

Nick Howe is an active contributor to the Tesla Motors forum, and is widely recognized in the Tesla community for his knowledge of Model S. He took delivery of his pearl white Performance 85 Model S in January 2013.

You can find him everywhere on the Internet (including the Tesla forums) as @nickjhowe